Early Childhood Education Series

Leslie R. Williams, Editor

(continued)

Everyday Goodbyes

Starting School
and
Early Care

A GUIDE TO THE SEPARATION PROCESS

NANCY BALABAN

Teachers College
Columbia University
New York and London

Published by Teachers College Press, 1234 Amsterdam Avenue, NY 10027

Library of Congress Cataloging-in-Publication Data

Balaban, Nancy, 1928–
    Everyday goodbyes : starting school and early care : a guide to the separation process / Nancy Balaban.
        p. cm. — (Early childhood education series)
    Includes bibliographical references and index.
    ISBN-13: 978-0-8077-4639-4 (pbk. : alk. paper)
    ISBN-10: 0-8077-4639-8 (pbk. : alk. paper)
    1. Readiness for school.   2. Separation (Psychology)   3. Separation anxiety in children.   I. Title.   II. Early childhood education series (Teachers College Press)

    LB1132.B338 2005
    372.21—dc22

                                                                        2005053808

ISBN-13:   ISBN-10:
978-0-8077-4639-4 (paper)   0-8077-4639-8 (paper)

Printed on acid-free paper

Manufactured in the United States of America

13   12   11   10   09   08   07   06   8   7   6   5   4   3   2   1

To Dorothy

When my youngest daughter went to kindergarten an event took place that caused her daily distress. The teacher, it seems, put Willie in the coat room every morning because he cried for his mother. He was permitted back into the classroom when he stopped crying. Eventually he learned not to cry for his mother.

This book is written in the belief that other solutions to Willie's crying can be found.

Contents

Preface

ARE YOU ABLE to remember your first day at school or child care?

Were you excited? Were you frightened? Were you sad?

Were you given a special pencil case or lunch box? Did you wear a shiny new pair of shoes?

Can you call up in your mind's eye your family saying goodbye? Did you climb onto a yellow school bus with a pounding heart or a lump in your throat?

Do these remembrances of the first day come back with an aura of excitement? Do they come back with the sting of fear or worry? Do they come back with a bittersweet mixture of both?

Do you recall any small details of that school beginning long ago: a curtained kindergarten window, a sandbox, a unfamiliar child with curly hair, boxes of large crayons, a shiny linoleum floor, the teacher's face or voice? Are there any memories of standing by the child care or kindergarten door, of trying out a new toy, of fighting back tears as your parent left? Are there flashes of newness or of strangeness?

Even though these memories are veiled by many years, they are often available to us as adults.

Beginning school or child care is an important event.

This work about beginning school or early care is offered as an aid to teachers and parents in the profound belief that this significant occasion can be a source of positive growth for everyone involved—children, teachers, and parents.

Acknowledgments

THIS BOOK was originally written as part of an Ed.D. dissertation for New York University.

I wish to acknowledge the assistance and influence of a number of people: the late Mary Allison, William Ayers, Sultana Christie, Sister Pat Dittmer, Amy Dombro, Ellen Dublin, Vanessa Duncan, Ellen Friedman, Dina Gabriel, Ellen Galinsky, the late Harriett Glassman, Carmen Hawthorne, Elisabeth Hirsch, the late William Hooks, Judith Johnson, Valerie Kennedy, Dana Levy, Lois Melman, Susan Merrick, Lorelle Phillips, Heather Prince-Clarke, B. J. Richards, the late Jose Rivera, Jane Rosenberg, Leigh Schuerholz, Molly Sexton, Marcine Weiner, Zenola Williams, and Pam Wheeler-Civita.

Parents, though anonymous, were generous in answering my questionnaires. Many students at Bank Street College contributed anecdotal records of children upon which I drew heavily, and some of which are quoted herein. Their accuracy and careful recording were an important source.

This work could not have been accomplished without the insights of the late Dr. Dorothy Gross, the late Dr. Henriette Glatzer, Dr. Virginia Casper, and the support, encouragement, and understanding of my late husband, Richard Crohn. Finally, I wish to thank my editor Susan Liddicoat, who waited for me and provided her supportive, creative, and thoughtful ideas.

This   is   when   my   Mommy   left   me .

Michele

1

Starting Early Care and Education: How Does It Feel?

IT IS 1951, and summer has come to a steady, hot, quiet hum
late in August . . . making way for anticipation of my first day
of kindergarten . . . [In] an open shoe box, with white tissue
paper unfolded enough to see them, are my new red school
shoes. [The] night before going to bed . . . I would put them on
the floor next to my feet and think, "I am going to school. I'm
going to step up the big high steps onto scary Mr. Gurky's scary
big school bus where I've heard the big kids chant, "Kindergarten
baby, stick your head in gravy" when the little kids get on. I'm
going to real school in a strange new place. *Will anybody know
who I am?*

P. L. Wehmiller, 2002, pp. 5–6

How does a young child feel going to early care and education for the
first time?
How do parents feel?
How do teachers feel on those first days?

Children, parents, and teachers all have a vast array of feelings about beginning school or group care.[1] A look at the nature of these feelings may
sharpen our focus on this event.

---

1. The term "parent" or "parents" is used in this book to denote the person who is the main caregiver for a child, such as a
mother, father, grandmother, aunt or uncle, older sibling, or foster parent.
    The words "early care and education," "center," and "school" are all used to indicate a range of settings including infant/
toddler and preschool child care centers, nursery schools for 2- to 4-year-olds, and kindergartners.

WHAT MIGHT CHILDREN BE FEELING?

Separation from parents or a primary caregiver frequently makes young children unhappy. They often feel abandoned, cast aside, and uncared for. They may be frightened and just as often angry. Sometimes children scream and cry. They throw things. They hit other children. They might try to hit the teacher. They bite. They kick. They lie on the floor and have temper tantrums.

Sometimes the situation is very different. A child walks into the classroom as if she belongs there, as if she has been there a thousand times before. She handles the equipment. She plays with other children. She blithely waves goodbye to her parent. She speaks in a friendly way with the teacher. "What a great kid!" we say. "No problem at all. Just left her mother and got really involved in the program." Then one day, her mother leaves as usual, and the girl collapses into a torrent of tears. No one can console her. She wants no part of any activity. Her behavior is completely unexpected. Her parents and her teachers feel bewildered and frustrated.

Other children may hide their feelings even more. They appear quiet and nonassertive. They seem to walk parallel to the life of the classroom. Often they are overlooked because they do not cause trouble. They seem self-sufficient and unassuming. A closer look may reveal that they are not involved with the materials of the program nor with other children to any significant degree. A teacher might think that such a child is mildly unhappy or has a low-key disposition. The parent may say he does not act that way at home. Such a child might be physically at school but psychologically at home.

Children usually show some reaction to the newness and the strangeness of an unfamiliar place. Some become agitated and race around the room, poking, prodding, touching, and looking. Others seem to be uncomfortable; they hang back and explore with their eyes while their bodies remain inert.

Not every child who comes into a classroom is affected in adverse ways. Some 4- and 5-year-olds march in full of confidence and behave as if they naturally belong in the room (seldom so with infants and toddlers). For them the first day of school may be the culmination of a summer of anticipation or the reality of a longed-for adventure, shared originally, perhaps, with an older sibling. Some may be quite used to school or group care through prior experiences, although this may have the opposite effect for certain children who did not work through their separation feelings the first time around. Others seem to enjoy the novelty of the situation, the excitement of being with other children their own age, and the pleasure of new playthings. However, most children react vigorously in some way to new surroundings, though that reaction may go undetected. It seems that children do mental and emotional work to absorb and understand a novel setting.

Children who feel sad or troubled about leaving the person or persons to whom they are attached do not always make those feelings known to the teacher.

Children need to size up the human environment as well as the physical environment when they enter a new classroom or group setting. The caregiver or teacher becomes an object of intense interest and curiosity. They wonder: Does the caregiver speak my language? Is the teacher my color? Are any of the caregiver's mannerisms or attitudes familiar? Are the teacher's reactions to my behavior like my parents' reactions?

These are especially important questions for children age birth to 2, whose identity is in the process of formation:

> Part of what infants and toddlers get from caregivers are perceptions of how people act at various times and in various situations (seen as how the infants should behave), how people act toward them and others (seen as how they and others should be treated) and how emotions are expressed (seen as how they should feel). The infant uses these impressions and often incorporates them into the self she becomes. (Lally, 1995, p. 59)

Factors like these contribute to a child's sense of strangeness or comfort because young children tend to define the whole adult world in terms of the behavior of their own family. Children often expect that all adults will behave as do the adults in their world. For example, if Mother leaves every morning in a rush to catch the bus and Grandma makes tortillas while singing, chances are that the young child believes that all mothers and grandmothers do that in the morning. If Father does not allow water play in the bathroom sink, the child may believe that all adults prohibit this sort of play and might even be surprised that it is an everyday activity in the center.

Children's identity is secured through the language they speak and the culture in which they are immersed. Children in out-of-home care or in school are frequently cared for by adults from cultures other than their own, who speak a different language. If a mother says hello in Spanish, and the teacher answers in English, she gives a message that "Spanish is unacceptable" (Chang, Muckelroy, & Pulido, 1996, p. 91). This is not lost on even the youngest children. So it is critical that teachers learn key words in the family's language. An infant teacher reported that when she spoke Spanish to 6- and 7-month-olds whose home language was Spanish, "They would look at me very intently, or respond with their bodies differently than when I spoke English" (p. 92). This was reassuring for the family as well as the child because they knew their language was supported and valued. Contrary to popular opinion, families should be encouraged to speak their home language with their children because knowing the home language well "is an excellent springboard into a second language" (p. 105). Since there is some concern that minority language children who are cared for in English are at risk for losing their home language (Wong-Fillmore, 1991), it is logical for many programs to make every effort to hire qualified ethnically and culturally diverse staff.

In sum, children come to group care or school with a set of expectations about adults built on their experiences. It takes time and new experiences with a variety of caring adults to teach them that adults behave in many different ways.

Because children enter early care and school with these preconceived notions about adults, they may be very uncomfortable as they begin to perceive that the teacher does not behave like their mother, father, or grandmother. Perhaps the teacher says it is fine to play with play dough, or talk while you eat, or get your hands dirty and sticky with glue. Children need time to put this new category of adult into their working intellectual and emotional scheme. They need time to differentiate between what goes on at home and what goes on at school. They need time to learn about the teacher, to learn what certain tones of voice mean, and to learn what to expect in various situations. They need time to sort out the differences between their teacher's and parents' behaviors. If the teacher is a benign, sensitive, and caring person, a child who is ready for school or group care will be able to transfer feelings of "basic trust" (Erikson, 1963) from home to the program.

When a child trusts, she transfers her loving feelings from parents to teachers.

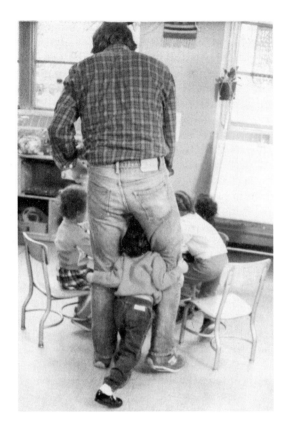

Until children come to feel this sense of trust, however, the teacher and the classroom remain strange. Day by day, familiarity replaces the unknown. This gradual process begins with the relationship between teacher and children. As children perceive the teacher in ever more trusting terms, they often begin to expand their relationships to the physical environment and to other children more openly. Establishing comfort with the teacher as a base enables children to become comfortable with the whole classroom. Children who have a secure relationship with their kindergarten teacher have been shown to be more outgoing, to play successfully with their peers, and do better in first and second grade (Elicker & Fortner-Wood, 1995).

Other research has revealed a similar process in infants (Bell, 1970). Babies, it seems, first need to know that people are trustworthy and here to stay. They gradually learn that their parent is not out of the world when out of sight. After that, babies are able to extend that concept to the physical objects in their world. It is by means of consistent, intimate human relationships that children become related to the larger physical and human world. Infants and toddlers who have secure relationships with their nonparental caregivers show an ability for greater self-regulation and less need for discipline strategies (Howes, 2000).

Can infants and toddlers in out-of-home care be assured of having such trustworthy and secure relationships? Yes, when the center director carefully designs and supports a *primary caregiving system,* in which each caregiver is assigned primary, daily, responsibility for a very small group of children. This does not mean that the caregiver cares *exclusively* for the same three children; rather that she has *principal* responsibility for the few children in her direct care.

This arrangement, which requires both serious staff commitment and dedicated planning, allows each baby and toddler to build a close, intimate bond with a particular person—in other words, an attachment. The baby knows who to go to for comfort, who will welcome him when saying goodbye to his parent, who will feed, change his diaper, put him down for a nap. The parent can talk about her baby with a caregiver who understands the baby well. In addition to "feelings of pride and achievement" (Howes, 2000, p. 74), the caregiver has the satisfaction of a meaningful relationship with both baby and parent. Primary caregiving, by providing a secure base for the baby, eases a child's anxiety and reassures the parent during

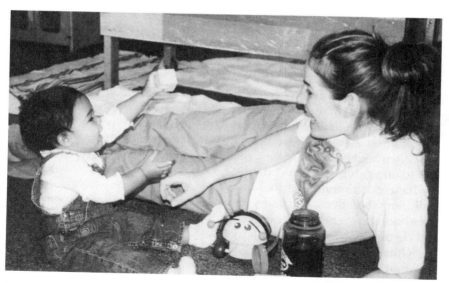

Primary caregiving brings the pleasure of a close relationship.

the transition from home care to center care. Teamwork among caregivers is absolutely essential for the system to run smoothly and effectively (Bernhardt, 2000), as the following anecdote reveals.

> Ms. Hsu arrives in the morning with eight-month-old Henry in her arms. She enters the room and is greeted by Patrice, Henry's primary caregiver. They discuss the breakfast and lunch she has brought in for him and then she and Henry play on the rug while Patrice attends to some other children. After about ten minutes, Ms. Hsu tells Patrice that she needs to leave soon. Patrice joins them on the rug for a few minutes playing with Henry before his mom announces to him that she is going to leave. They stand up and Ms. Hsu hands him over to Patrice's arms. He goes willingly, but keeps his eyes focused on his mom. Mom says to Henry, "I'm going to leave. I'm going to work. I'll be back later." She gives him a kiss, walks to the door, and waves goodbye. Patrice helps Henry wave his hand. He looks at Patrice and frowns ever so slightly. Patrice sings to him, plays with him for a few minutes, and when he's comfortable, chewing on a toy, she attends to another child. After several minutes, Henry begins to fret. Another caregiver, Alice, notices his distress and sits close to him. He turns away from her. When she picks him up he begins to cry. When he spots Patrice he reaches out to her. Alice walks over to Patrice, hands him to her, saying, "Here's Patrice. She's right here." Henry quiets down and gives Patrice a big smile. Patrice cuddles him, "I'm right here."
>
> (P. Callaghan, from student journal, 2004)

Children may feel strange in a new group that is unlike the familiar family group in which they have a special status. Few people know their names. No one knows whether they like vanilla ice cream or chocolate, or what frightens or comforts them. No one really likes or dislikes them in any particular way. Three- to 5-year-olds, unlike infants and toddlers, are interested in becoming members of the peer group. They will have to earn acceptance through their behavior. While they do not know this yet, perhaps they sense it.

Children may worry that no one will take care of them, that they will not know how to get home, that they will not be able to find their parents, or that their parents will not be able to find them. The younger the child, the more intense these feelings of fear. Marisol, 25 months, steadfastly refused to leave the child care room to go to the park because "Papi no find me." Some research concludes that until children are around 3 years old, they cannot retain a stable inner mental image of their absent parents (Mahler,

Pine, & Bergman, 1975). Words or explanations of parental whereabouts are often ineffective with such young children until they trust the new adult. Infants and toddlers need concrete reminders of their families' existence such as photographs or some treasured object from home.

The way children approach separation may also be determined by their particular individual or cultural family style. One family may be flamboyant; goodbyes and other emotional events may be treated in a demonstrative fashion. Another family may be more reserved; their feelings are not openly revealed and meaningful events are handled with outward composure.

> A Chinese boy came to pre-k clinging to his father, head buried in his shoulder. He would not allow his father to enter the room with him, but agreed to stay in the doorway each morning. After several days and many teacher peekaboos, he agreed to come in, still velcrolike on his outwardly unruffled father.

The transition to early care and education is a scenario composed of the personal/cultural expectations and experiences of a large cast of characters of all ages. Sometimes the interactions result in a lively production, with adults and children supporting one another's roles. Other interactions may need more rehearsals to smooth out the rough edges. How parents are feeling is a significant part of this drama.

WHAT MIGHT PARENTS BE FEELING?

Sometimes teachers say that it is not the child who is having trouble separating but the parent. Surely a child's feelings are intimately bound up with those of his mother or father. Parents may have various kinds of emotions when they bring their children to school or child care for the first time. It is not possible to understand a child's feelings without simultaneously acknowledging the parent's feelings. Entry to school or care is a significant event for both.

Parents may wonder: Can this teacher really take care of my child? Will the caregiver understand him when he makes requests? Will the teacher like her? What will the caregiver do if my child misbehaves? Will she humiliate me or enhance me in the eyes of the teacher? Will he reveal things about our family that are private? What will happen if my child gets hurt in school? Can I really trust this caregiver with her? These nagging questions make it difficult for some parents to hand over their son or daughter to a teacher's care.

Parents may worry about how their children will get along without them or how they will function without parental control, guidance, or protection. In situations where parents have not left their children outside the home before, this feeling may be particularly strong. In some cases it may be less worrisome if this is a second or third child. Alternatively, a parent may expect the separation to go more smoothly with a second or third child and that may not be the case. However, more depends on a child's personality and relationship with the parents than the birth order.

One source of this worry may be the parents' ambivalence. On the one hand, they want their children to go to school or to child care. It gives them some much-needed time away from their children—time for themselves or time to pursue their work. Sometimes parents, normally, want to "get rid of" their children. They may secretly want to experience life as it was before they were parents. On the other hand, they love their children and wish to keep them near, to protect them, and to make sure all goes well with them. These ambivalent feelings are often uncomfortable for parents. When school begins, they may worry unduly about their children as a means of covering up, to themselves, their feelings of joy in their newfound freedom.

Parents may have other concerns as well. They may worry about the teacher's competence. The teacher is, after all, a stranger, and it is not easy to leave a baby or young child with a stranger. Why should a parent trust an unknown entity? Why should parents believe that a teacher or caregiver will take as good care of their daughter or son as they would? Parents need some hard evidence that their children are in truly good hands to alleviate this worry.

What might this parent be feeling as she bids goodbye to her daughter?

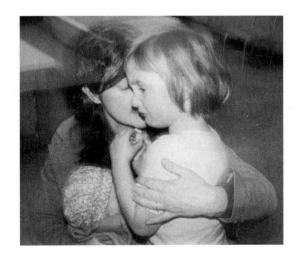

Parents may also feel jealousy. "Suppose the teacher takes better care of Delores than I do?" "What if Dwayne loves the caregiver more than me?" Parents may find it hard to willingly entrust their children to a potentially conflict-ridden situation.

> Candace brings her 6-week-old infant to child care, having visited several times before. She spends a long time fixing up the baby's crib. She explains the infant's routine to the caregiver and says she will be back to nurse her. She kisses the baby and leaves. As she goes out the door, she puts her hands over her face, shaking with sobs. The caregiver puts an arm around her for comfort and tells her to call anytime. After a month, she withdraws the baby because she doesn't want to miss any of her baby's "firsts."
>
> (A. Sanger, from student journal, 2002)

Parents may further be concerned that they, as good parents, will be unmasked. "Suppose the teacher finds out that Paola is not really the great creative genius that I believe she is?" What if the teacher discovers the child's flaws—that she is a thumb-sucker, he wets the bed, she kicks and bites, he uses fresh language, she is disobedient? "Will the teacher see me as a bad parent when she discovers these traits in my child?" Parents often feel that they will be judged by the teacher when they first bring their child to group care or school.

Some of these parental feelings are understandable when they are examined in the light of the parents' own histories. Parents themselves were once children in school. Perhaps they, like their own children, were shy or fearful about initially going to school. Parents also have feelings about teachers that are based on those past experiences. These feelings often resurface at school beginnings when parents recapture some of their own experiences with entry and separation. Feelings of fear, anxiety, worry, and discomfort mixed with excitement are to be expected as parents enter a classroom with their children for the first time.

An Informal Survey of Parents' Feelings

I sent a questionnaire to a group of 44 parents whose children, aged 10 months to 4 years, were in three different child care centers. The parents were Black, White, and Hispanic, male and female, and their socioeconomic status ranged from factory workers and maintenance workers to college professors, doctors, and lawyers. I asked them three questions:

1. What were your feelings when you knew that your child would soon be entering school or group care?

2. How did you feel the first day you accompanied your child to school or group care?
3. How did you feel about the separation from your child and your child's being in the teacher's care after the first few weeks had gone by?

Of the 22 who replied, many parents said they had mixed feelings when they knew their children would be entering group care. While they felt good because they knew, from friends or from experience, that the center was a safe and trustworthy place, they also felt worried about a variety of matters. Some worried about leaving their children. They wrote:

Was she too young at 14 months? Would she become depressed or more clinging because of the separation?
My first feeling was that we were going to be apart for a couple of hours each day.
Sadness and loss that he was getting older and separating more from me.
How would she adapt being out of the closeness with me?

Some parents were concerned about their children's behavior:

Would she perform well?
I started thinking about how he would react when told to do something. How he would act when told to settle down the same time the other children do. My feelings are very deeply concerned with him being able to function correctly.

Other parents were troubled about the teacher's competence.

He's only 7 months—will the caregivers know what it means when he cries? They gave him bananas for the first time. Is it OK for him?
My son (21 months) has Down Syndrome. I want his care to be done my way, though I try to get over that. The teachers are so young—how would they know what to do? But I needed a break and he needs contact with other children.

Some of the parents reported they were entirely positive about beginning group care for their children, but one commented, "Well, I wasn't happy because it was really the first time she would be away from me for a few hours a day, outside of her being with my family."

In describing their feelings when they actually accompanied their children to a center, parents used words such as "nervous," "anxious," "sad," "worried," "apprehensive," "tense," and "strange." All the parents, except one, admitted to these emotions. Two said they thought they felt more nervous than their children did. Several stated that they felt it was a "loss," a "milestone," "a big change that she was starting to grow away from me." Several expressed very strong feelings:

> It was very hard for me to leave, and I had tears in my eyes.
> I also missed my child a lot. I felt anxious about what would happen in the new surroundings.
> I didn't feel too good because I wasn't used to leaving my daughter with people I really didn't know.
> I felt a little jealous—some days I felt guilty—she's only a baby. It's hard to see your child snuggle up to her teacher or light up when I take her to the center.
> Even though it's hard to see her have a grand old time, at the same time it's also a relief to see her happy there.

One parent told of a friend whose toddler woke up at night and asked for his caregiver. Others expressed their worry about leaving a daughter or son with strangers. One parent wrote, "It's a little bit difficult for the parents because they are entrusting people they still don't know very well with what is most precious to them—their child."

Some parents made connections with their own experiences with separation. One wrote that she felt "Nervous. Excited. Apprehensive. Thrilled. It brought back fond memories of my first day of school—a day I had eagerly awaited for many months." Another felt "somewhat sad and tearful about leaving her this time and thinking about all the other partings in the future—and past, I'll bet."

One parent of a 20-month-old recalled the third day:

> It was probably the most traumatic for us both. I left the school after dropping him off. He cried miserably. I went home to clean the house in a torrent of tears and guilt for being a part of a society that uproots babies from their mothers at such a young age. That afternoon, when I picked him up, he was listening to a story. We both cried and embraced after a long separation.

After the first few weeks had gone by, all the parents said they felt better. They used words such as "wonderful," "confident," "relieved," "secure," "positive," "comfortable," and "fine." These positive feelings built up because the separation was gradual and they saw that their children were happy. "She liked it, so I felt wonderful because the teachers treated her fine and she was happy with the other kids." "Yet in time," another wrote, "I learned that she just enjoyed it here very much. The teachers were supportive and wonderful to me as well as my child." Another summed up many of the other parents' feelings when she wrote, "As soon as a child shows signs of happiness, one feels relieved."

Trust in the staff seemed to be at the core of parents' resolution of their anxious feelings:

> I felt that he was in good hands.
> I felt much better than I had anticipated. This was just another step but nothing anxious or worrisome. I trusted the staff.

Several parents wrote about the support toward growth. "I still enjoy our times together," one parent said, "reading, playing, and experiencing new things, but we are both happier being able to grow in our separate ways." Just because parents feel less worried after the separation has been tested and tried does not seem to mean that the initial feelings disappear entirely. One parent wrote, touchingly:

> I still wonder if I've made the right choice. There are times during the day when I miss her very much. But it is a great comfort to me that she is so near where I work and I can readily go to see her and that she is in the care off such a wonderful staff. I think I would come to visit even more often, but the thought of coming and then leaving again sometimes deters me. As you can see, I'm not very good at partings.

WHAT MIGHT TEACHERS BE FEELING?

Some teachers feel tremendously confident when the program begins. They may feel excited at the prospect of meeting a new group of children, or might feel nervous about the first days. Some might worry about what to do with possible criers or have concern about how long their crying will last. Often teachers feel uncomfortable being around many parents for several days or may experience feelings of anger at parents who seem "pushy" or others who seem uncaring. For many teachers, having parents in the room for any length of time may be unpleasant and might find themselves wishing they could move them out as soon as possible. A caregiver might not look forward to the first few days because of the strain and emotional drain it causes. Once the routines are established and children are comfortable, teachers might breathe a sight of relief and feel that finally they can get down to the business of teaching.

There is nothing unusual about teachers feeling some of the same worries and discomforts that children and their parents are experiencing. Just

When a teacher remains calm and supportive, she gives a child the opportunity to recover from the upset of separation.

as parents were once children in school, so were teachers. They have memories of their own school beginnings, some of which were positive and some probably not. These memories contribute to the feelings that are aroused as teachers and parents become involved in first-day activities.

All of us, teachers, as well as parents, have had personal experiences with several other forms of separation, such as graduation, vacations, changing jobs, moving, divorce, marriage, or death. How we were affected by any of these situations in the past may influence how we feel and behave in the classroom when the program begins.

Other feelings, especially those related to parents, may be a source of difficulty for teachers and caregivers. These emotions may cause teachers to be eager for parents to leave the room, even before the children are ready to let them go. Teachers may find themselves at odds with some parents and in conflict with them about what is best for a child. Dealings with parents often arouse in teachers feelings they have, or had, about their own parents.

A group of teachers participating in a workshop on separation was asked to think of a word they associated with the word "separation." Here are some of their responses:

Fear	Angry	Help
Anxiety	Venturing forth	Distance
Pain	Out of control	Unhappy
Alone	Rejection	

For almost all, "separation" conjured up a collection of feelings that were raw and unsettling. When discussing their responses, they explored the reasons for such unhappy associations. Their personal experiences with separation seemed to be the most potent molder of their present feelings—how their parents treated them when there was a separation. "I was told to be a big girl and not to cry. I was probably only four or five years old," one participant recalled.

They also saw past stressful events, such as the birth of a sibling or their own parents' absence from home for an extended period of time, as influences on their present feelings. Some found that striking out on their own and venturing forth were gratifying separation experiences that led to intellectual expansion and new levels of self-confidence.

Perhaps if teachers and caregivers are able to examine their own feelings when school begins or when a new child enters the center for the first time, a connection to some of the emotions described here will be revealed. Once teachers are able to understand some of their own feelings, they may be more alert to similar feelings in parents and children.

THE IMPACT OF SEPARATION IS COMPLEX

Separation affects children. It affects parents. It arouses feelings in teachers. School beginnings can be exciting as well as uncomfortable occasions. Along with those who are genuinely delighted to be starting school or child care, there are frequently crying children, accompanied by tense and nervous parents. Often teachers feel pulled by the conflicting needs of the children, the demands of the parents, and their own inclinations. Parents express their concerns:

> Where shall I put her sweater?
> Could I have a few words with you privately about Melissa? She's a very sensitive child.
> Where will the bus leave him off?
> Please don't let her drink grape juice. It stains her clothes.

Children wail:

> Mommy. I want my mommy. Where's my mommy?

By the end of the first day, a teacher's head may be spinning from the accumulated problems and concerns of the children and parents, mixed with the excitement of a new group and a new year ahead. A situation that provokes so many feelings and so many memories is bound to produce reactions in all who are involved.

2

The Meanings of Separation

SEPARATION IS AN experience that occurs in all phases of human life. It starts at birth when the infant leaves the known, 9-month inner home for the strange outer world of bright lights, sounds, and the touch of human skin. It is seen in the wobbling of toddlers, practicing separation as they scoot away from a beckoning parent. Preschoolers experience separation as they leave the security of the home to enter an unknown world of the school. School-age children mourn the loss of friends who move away. Separation characterizes many events in developing adult life—an adolescent breaks up with a girlfriend or boyfriend; a young adult graduates from college and charts a new course; adults move to a new home; a person changes jobs; someone gets married, another gets divorced; a spouse dies.

All these events are bound by a common thread. In each circumstance, an individual is leaving familiar territory and entering the unknown, the untried. A potential for growth and change exists in every separation experience even though a temporary sense of loss predominates. Few people set out on a new venture without thoughts of what they have left behind.

Sometimes ceremony lessens the impact of a loss by acknowledging a particular separation as a legitimate transition to a new phase of development. In some primitive cultures rituals such as shaving a child's head may symbolize cutting him off from his past connections and indicate his entry into another stage of life. Spanking at a birthday party may be an old-fashioned counterpart of this custom. In an elaborate ceremony in some Hispanic communities, a 15-year-old girl, wearing a floor-length dress, makes her debut before church and society in a rite of passage from childhood to adulthood known as *quinceañera*. Other present-day events such as baptisms, bar and bat mitzvahs, graduations, and weddings mark the transition from one stage of life to another.

Entering early care and education is a transition to a new stage for children as well as parents, but there is no unique ritual that is culturally shared. A new lunch box, a pair of new shoes, a pencil case, or a new jacket or cap may be symbols to mark an event that is full of meaning and possibilities for children, parents, and teachers. Yet they share no tradition to ease them through this important occasion.

In many early childhood settings teachers introduce their own rituals to help children feel secure and comfortable. Some send notes of welcome to children's homes prior to opening day. They label cubbies with a child's name or post a list of children's names with their birthdays to welcome the newcomers. Usually teachers sing songs or play games that focus on each child's name. Teachers of infants and toddlers might take photographs of the child and parent during the phase-in period and post them in an easy-to-see spot. These photos help babies remember that their absent parents still exist. Bringing a few flowers (or the proverbial apple) to the teacher or a special snack for classmates might be a family's way to mark this first day event.

ATTACHMENT: THE ROOTS OF SEPARATION FEELINGS

Many young children display strong reactions when they are separated, or even anticipate separation, from their parents. Where do the roots of these feelings lie?

There is evidence that the roots are very deep. They lie in the stable, deep, and abiding attachment between parents and children that is usually formed during the first year of life. Small (1998) defines attachment as "wanting to be with one another, feeling comfortable in someone's presence, falling in love. And so attachment to parents, offspring, mates, and kin is the norm for us and we expect to have all sorts of attachments throughout life" (pp. 14–15). It is this attachment that prompts a parent to rush to the bedside of a sick child, though the "child" be an adult, the parent elderly, and the distance many miles.

Even beyond the child's first year of life, adoptive and foster parents are able to form an attachment. Babies appear to have a capability to become attached to a responsive, caring adult (Dozier, Albus, Stoval, & Bates, 2001). Research has revealed no differences in attachment between adoptive and nonadoptive mother-infant pairs when the children were between 13 and 18 months (Singer, Brodzinsky, Ramsay, Steir, & Waters, 1985).

The term *attachment* has special meaning. It is not the same as *dependence*. Although the two terms are often used interchangeably, they are significantly different from each other. Children who are securely attached to their parents have an abiding trust in their parents' reliability, which fosters their own burgeoning self-reliance and self-confidence (Ainsworth,

Many attachment relationships are characterized by trust.

Bell, & Stayton, 1974). Children who are dependent, it is thought, sidestep their own thrusts toward autonomy and lean on their parents instead. According to John Bowlby (1969), author of the seminal work on separation, *dependence*, which refers to an infant's state of helplessness, is present at its "maximum at birth and diminishes more or less steadily until maturity is reached, [whereas] attachment is altogether absent at birth and is not strongly in evidence until after an infant is past six months" (p. 228). He further describes dependency in human relations as a condition to be avoided and attachment as a condition to be cherished.

However, Eastern countries—such as Japan, Korea, China, have a different cultural perspective that does not regard dependency as a negative characteristic. It is incorporated in the word *amae*, which does not exist in Western languages. According to Young-Bruehl and Bethelard (2000), *amae* implies that people are born with the expectation or the wish to be loved. The word conveys the idea of "leaning on another," which these authors embody in the word "cherishment." "Cherishment," they state, "is spontaneous affection . . . located right in the roil and broil of emotional life, in the growth and development of a self . . . We now easily think of cherishment as the emotional equivalent of nourishment. Soul food" (p. 9).

Frequently young children, who tightly hold their parents' body or hide in their clothing when entering an unfamiliar early care and education setting, are regarded by teachers as dependent rather than as attached. However, such actions are legitimate, inborn attachment behaviors that keep infants and young children close to their parents. Clinging, crying, calling, or following are characteristic of all young humans and are explained by ethologists (those who study the connections between human and animal life) as remnants of an urgent, primitive, protective mechanism.

Attachment relationships are not only defined by clinging or crying. Many are embroidered with smiles and joyous exchanges when parents and children strike a comfortable balance with one another. These children seem to have an intuitive understanding and faith in their parents' predictability. They seem to know each other well and to trust one another's behavior.

Although attachment of children to their parents or prime caretaker is universal (Vanljzendoorn & Sagi, cited in Cassidy & Shaver, 1999), cultural values dictate how parents perceive specific attachment behaviors. In a study of Anglo and Puerto Rican mothers, Harwood and Miller (1991) found that "Anglo mothers placed more emphasis on self-confidence, independence, and the ability to function autonomously. In contrast, Puerto Rican mothers focused more on obedience, the capacity for relatedness, and the maintenance of proper demeanor" (p. 583).

Many parents in Western cultures aim to foster individuality and independence, while parents in the majority of the world's cultures value family ties, closeness, and interdependence. Lubeck refers to these "two patterns [as] . . . a collective orientation versus an individualistic orientation" (Lubeck, 1985, cited in Gonzalez-Mena, 2005, p. 90). People in cultures that value kinship, embeddedness, and community see the self as connected to the group for life. Parents aspire to teach their children that they are interdependent on one another and a parent from such a culture might discourage a child from wanting to "do it myself." A Vietnamese college student recalled that her mother spoon-fed her until first grade (but insisted that she do her own homework). In a video about diverse child-rearing customs, a Japanese mother is shown feeding her 2-year-old then, in turn, feeding her 4-year-old who is sitting beside her. African-American, Hmong, and Vietnamese families, among others, express this cultural viewpoint through child rearing practices such as shared child care, cosleeping of children and their parents, and multigenerational households (Janet Gonzalez-Mena, personal communication, October 18, 2002).

These orientations are so much a part of family life that parents may not be aware that these are not ubiquitous points of view. They may be surprised to see how many ways children and parents separate when school or care begins. In an urban kindergarten African-American children have been known to arrive for the first day with grandma, mother, an aunt, a big sister or brother, or all four, whereas White suburban children tend to arrive with one parent or caregiver.

Staff development focused on the wide variety of cultural practices is needed to sharpen teachers' awareness of their own, as well as others', culture. Carlson and Harwood (2000) describe a situation in which a teacher (individualistic style) tries to persuade a parent (collective style) to allow her toddler to feed herself. When her efforts fail, the teacher, with the aid of a consultant, is able to arrive at a compromise with the parent.

It is not unusual for teachers or caregivers to assume that the values they hold are shared by the families and children in their care. Yet becoming alert to others' ideas of what behavior is important for young children is a necessity in our increasingly diverse society. Chang with Pulido (1994) challenge us to recognize that

> It is easy for even the most culturally sensitive person to inadvertently teach a child culturally inappropriate behavior. Consider the experience of one infant/toddler caregiver who, despite her own bilingual (English/Spanish) and bicultural background (Mexican American), found she was unable to anticipate a cross-cultural issue which arose for a Korean toddler under her care. Noticing that the 18-month-old allowed other toddlers to take away her toys, . . . the provider patiently worked to teach the girl to be more assertive and to hold on to her toys . . . Watching this new behavior, [the parents] exclaimed, "What will we do when we return to Korea? Such selfishness is unacceptable!" (pp. 13–14)

Since most early childhood programs in this country value independence and individualism, it is a formidable task for teachers to distinguish a "collective" cultural style from dependence. In order to embrace both major cultural patterns, perhaps teachers should think about separation and attachment not only as a child's movement *away* from a parent but also as movement *toward* a connection with others (Kestenberg-Amigi, 2004).

HOW ATTACHMENT DEVELOPS

Although there are speculations that bonding may begin immediately after birth, a wide variety of experiences must occur between infants and their parents before attachment becomes secure. Two pediatricians, Marshall Klaus and John Kennell (1976), postulated the existence of a sensitive period immediately after birth in which babies and their parents were predisposed to bonding.[1] Their research prompted them to conclude that this bonding was essential for parent-child attachment and had far-reaching consequences. While these findings have aroused controversy (Lamb, 1982; Lamb & Hwang, 1982), and qualification by Klaus and Kennell (1982) themselves, the idea that early and extended parent-infant contact is important has influenced hospitals to change maternity practices in an effort to be more humane. Whether or not early and extended contact affects the quality of attachment remains to be seen, but the fact that more parents and their newborns even in their short hospital stay are permitted to remain together to strengthen the attachment process is noteworthy.

A baby may "belong" to its parents in the parents' view, however, long before the parents truly "belong" to the baby, according to Margaret Mahler (Mahler, Pine, & Bergman, 1975). Through research about babies and their mothers, she evolved a theory about the development of young children's sense of self. She believes that for the first 2 or 3 months babies experience parents as extensions of themselves, unable to completely distinguish the boundaries that exist between them. A young baby is described as believing that the nipple containing milk appears in her mouth by magic, called up by her own desires to relieve her hunger pangs. If an infant could talk, she might say, "Oh, I'm so hungry. What I need is some milk. Ah, here's the nipple with milk. How powerful I am to make it come to me when I need it." Mahler defines this as babies' sense of their own omnipotence.

Daniel Stern (1985), who shares with Mahler an interest in the growing relationship of the baby and mother, has a different slant on how this develops because his concern is for the infant as a social being. His emphasis is on the emergence and development of a *sense of self* that *starts* at birth. He believes there are different aspects of this sense of self that enfold upon each other throughout life.

> I conclude that during the first two months the infant is actively forming a sense of an emergent self. It is a sense of organization in the process of formation, and it is a sense of self that will remain active for the rest of life. An overarching sense of self is not yet achieved in this period, but it is coming into being. (p. 38)

Mahler's theory states that at around 4 or 5 months of age a "hatching" takes place as babies begin to break out of the psychological shell that wrapped them and their parents together. Little by little they begin to per-

---

1. *Bonding* refers to the parent's feelings of concern and commitment toward the newborn infant, while *attachment* describes the enduring emotional tie between child and parent growing out of their day-to-day interactions.

ceive the difference between themselves and their parents and to know the parents' bodies as different from their own, the parents' faces as different from other faces. They begin to know and to prefer the parents.

Usually, by the middle of the first year, through intimate looking, touching, hearing, speaking, seeing, and by means of babies' own development, they have become attached to their parents (Schaffer & Emerson, 1964). They come to know that the parents are their own particular persons whose looks, smell, touch, and sound are special. This attachment is the basis of human relatedness from which children derive the capacity for strong feelings about important people. It is this that enables children to become friends and lovers, as well as enemies. There is recent evidence that attachment may be influenced not only by emotions but by biology in the form of an attachment hormone oxytocin (Carey, 2004). It seems that attachment is involved at the deepest level of the brain. "When we sense that the environment is safe, the release of oxytocin allows us to enjoy the comfort of an embrace without fear" (Porges, 2004, p. 21).

As infants grow and develop, their attachment to their parents becomes more complex, more laden with feelings and meanings for all involved. Evidence of the strength of this bond is seen at around 8 or 9 months of age when babies may recoil, hide their faces, or sometimes shriek at the sight of a strange or unknown person. It is as if the baby were saying to the stranger, "I really know the person whom I love best—and it's not you." This occurrence is often called "stranger anxiety." As a child continues to develop, aided by the secure, certain relationship of his or her parents, this intense reaction to strangers usually begins to fade.

In fact, toddlers between 10 and 15 or 16 months of age tend to be the very opposite of the suspicious 7- to 9-month-olds. They are like joyous world explorers, especially in the company of their parents. They have been described as having a "love affair with the world" (Greenacre, 1957). When not in the company of their parents, toddlers of this age often seem in low-key moods. They seem to be most free to explore when they have a secure base from which to roam. Mahler refers to toddlers of this age as "practicing" (Mahler, Pine, & Bergman, 1975). In practicing their newly acquired walking skills, they weave, wobble, and toddle, arms over head for balance. They freely wander off to see new and thrilling sights that have opened up to them, now that they are upright.

With this tremendous new scope to their lives also comes a particular danger, according to Mahler's theory. Their separateness from their parents is now a physical reality. They realize that they are vulnerable, that they still need care and protection. This realization often drives them back to the arms, laps, or legs of their parents for "emotional refueling" (Mahler,

Pine, & Bergman, 1975). It is often bewildering to the parents and to the caregivers of toddlers between 18 and 22 or 24 months of age that such formerly "independent" beings could become so clingy. This period, which Mahler calls the "rapprochement crisis," is frequently one of the most difficult periods for both parents and teachers (Resch, 1975; Rodriguez & Hignett, 1981), because, as Resch puts it, "all hell breaks loose" when children are left in group care or even at home with babysitters.

Not only are most children this age painfully aware of their need for their attachment person, but they are still developing the cognitive, as well as the emotional, ability to deal with that person's absence. While many children are able to call up in their mind's eye a "love memory" (Virginia Casper, personal communication, March 11, 2005) of that person by the time they are eighteen or twenty months old, that ability is not always reliable. This internal love memory develops out of the pleasurable, as well as the not so pleasurable experiences that the baby has, from birth on, with the main caregiver. The stability of that love memory is highly influenced by the toddler's emotions. Under tense, stressful conditions the memory is often harder to maintain than in relaxed, comfortable times. For toddlers, out of sight is often out of mind. It is very hard to bear. It may seem to these young children that the beloved, missed adult will never return. Prolonged crying, intense rage, and uncontrollable sobbing are common in 18- to 24-month-old toddlers. It is not surprising that parents and teachers often feel incompetent, frustrated, or even frequently angry at children in these circumstances.

When a toddler becomes a 2-year-old, the intensity of these attachment feelings continues to be aroused when separation occurs or is even suspected by a child. For a child of 20 to 24 or 26 months, separation can be especially difficult. By this age, children have attached significance and strong feelings to the departure of parents, and they often become inconsolable at separation, even those of short duration (Resch, 1975). Two-year-old children have a profound understanding of the importance of these special parent people. They know, deeply, their own tremendous need and reliance on them. This knowledge increases their terror and panic when that person leaves them. Translated into the language of a child, those feelings might be stated like this:

> I really know that you are my special person. I know that I need
> you to take care of me in all situations. I am afraid that if you leave
> me, I won't be able to take care of myself. It makes me angry that
> you want to go away like that, and I feel sad and hurt. So, in order
> not to feel that way, I'm going to do what I know how to do best to
> keep you here. I can cry. I can hold on to you, I can follow you, I can

call you. These things ought to work, because they've worked before.

That is what attachment has been described to mean to very young children.

ABOUT SEPARATING

As children grow into preschoolers of 3 and 4, separation reactions take a different form from those they had at age 2. For one thing, most children have completed the phase of their "second" or "psychological" birth (Mahler, Pine, & Bergman, 1975). They have emerged from infancy and toddlerhood with a clearer sense of themselves as individuals, attached to but distinctly separate from their parents. They are described as having attained a state of "constancy," which is "the enduring inner conviction of being me and nobody else" (Kaplan, 1978, p. 35).

Another reason that 3- and 4-year-olds may handle separation differently from 2-year-olds and toddlers is that they are able to consistently mentally represent their absent parents. As any adult knows, there is some comfort in being able to conjure up in your thoughts the person you are missing. Out of sight is no longer out of mind.

Being able to separate, becoming a "real school person" at 3, 4, and 5 is most gratifying and pleasurable for many young children. Often preschoolers are excited by the new environment replete with attractive playthings and a bevy of children their own age. Separation for these children is an adventure and a challenge. Eventually the ability to separate is a necessity if children are to develop as autonomous and self-reliant beings. It is a capacity that teachers applaud and most parents try to support. It is built up in preschool children through the cumulative separation experiences they have had, such as staying with friends, grandparents, other relatives, and sitters, and going to birthday parties or to visit in other children's homes.

However, the ability to tolerate the stress of separation and the ability to adjust to strange and new situations vary greatly from child to child. Not all 3-, 4-, or even 5-year-olds are able to enter school with complete comfort. Certain developmental abilities are needed. They have been cited by Anna Freud (1965) as necessary to a preschooler's competent entry to early education. She states that self-feeding and control of bowel and bladder are prerequisites because they indicate growing bodily independence. The ability to relate to other children and to accept them as partners in their own right, especially in make-believe play, plus the ability to use play materials in self-initiated and directed activities are further indications that young children can make the transition to early care and education.

> At eighteen months, Casey uses play to help develop the competencies needed to separate. Playing in the sand table, she picks up some plastic rocks and pushes them under the sand. She turns to the teacher and says, "Where rocks go?" She answers her own question by digging in the sand, pulling out the rocks, saying "Here!" She turns to her teacher and says, "Now you." Her teacher then hides them. Casey digs in the sand, jumps up and down, and with a huge smile, shouts "Here!"
>
> (D. Rosenbloom, from student journal, 2003).

In addition, Freud states that impulse control and the ability, at some times, to wait a turn, tolerate frustration, and express negative feelings appropriately are also necessary to ensure a child's successful entry into preschool.

We all know many children who, on entering school, fit these guidelines and are able to leave their parents with a minimum of stress. We also know other children who do not entirely fit these descriptions and for whom entry and continued presence in the early education setting is stressful and unsuccessful.

Since parents are largely the mediators of their young children's experiences, they help children understand the meaning of events and other people's behavior in the way they explain these to children and the way in which they, the parents, behave. Parents translate separation at school in many different ways and communicate a variety of ideas and feelings about the event to their children. Often these ideas and feelings are expressed through the attachment relationship, so it is not very easy for someone else, such as a teacher, to distinguish a secure attachment relationship from one that is insecure.

Children from Special Circumstances

One situation that lies outside this description occurs when children are in foster care or have been, or are, homeless. Then the process of adjusting to early care and education is especially poignant, because, like adopted children, they have undergone a major separation from their parents. A significant percent of children in foster care are under age 5, with those under age 1 constituting the fastest growing segment (Dozier, Dozier, & Manni, 2002). These children have intense needs for safety, security, affection, and reassurance and are most likely to face health and developmental challenges (Eheart & Zimmerman, 1998). Because of attachment difficulties, they often behave as though teachers and caregivers are not needed (Dozier et al., 2002). On the other hand, they may act overly friendly at first to the teacher who is still a stranger (Albus & Dozier, 1999). Such behaviors can be easily misunderstood and forming a relationship with children in these circumstances is challenging.

Adjustment to early care and education may be a long process for these children because their attachment issues demand special attention. Initially, some children may be cautious. Later, when they are comfortable, they may start testing and acting out, as if asking the question, "How much is the teacher going to be there for me?" (Klein, Bittel, & Molnar, 1993, p. 27). With this population, a primary caregiving system, as described in Chapter 1, is a necessity.

Teachers need support and consultation to help them recognize and respond to the underlying neediness of these children's often disruptive or puzzling behaviors. It is essential to respond to the children's distress and nurture them in order to provide "a predictable, responsive, interpersonal world [that] helps in the development of behavioral, emotional, and physiological regulation" (Dozier et al., 2002, p. 10).

These very stressed young children require a predictable and organized classroom environment, a staff who truly knows them, special attention at mealtimes and nap, regular and predictable routines, careful planning of transitions, and supported time for play (Garbarino, Dubrow, Kostelny, & Pardo, 1992, cited in Adams, 1995). Continuity of staff, a high staff-child ratio, small groups, and a well-organized schedule are priorities "because [the classroom] may be the singular refuge from a chaotic world" (Klein et al., 1993, p. 23).

Oddly enough, at the same time we say hello, especially to children who are homeless, we also need to be prepared to say goodbye. "The harsh reality is that from the moment a child arrives, dealing with goodbye must be a priority . . . many children leave the program without notice . . . so the curriculum must deal with goodbye and leaving on a continuous basis" (Klein et al., 1993, p. 28).

When a boy or girl who is homeless enters the program, it is a good time to start making a "goodbye" book. Include photographs of the child, alone and with her parent, engaged in activities with her teacher, and at play with friends. Allow for and encourage train, car, and bus play, complete with packing a suitcase, and waving goodbye.

Well-honed sensitivity is called for because children who are homeless, or are in foster care, may come from "ethnic and racial groups that are most different from and most excluded from mainstream society [and] live in two separate worlds: in their own enclaves and in the larger community" (Bowman, 1999, p. 292).

Transition to Kindergarten

Even though most 5-year-olds have been to preschool, child care, or family child care, going to kindergarten is the consummate "real and formal entry into elementary school" (Edson, 1994, p. 69). It is "a major life change for young children . . . [requiring adjustment to a] new peer group, a new role as 'student,' a new authority figure, and new expectations" (Maxwell & Eller, 1994, p. 56). Entry into kindergarten involves more than just the child's transition; "it is a process in which child, family, school, and community interrelate across time . . . in which the child's development is the key focus or goal" (Pianta & Cox, 1999, p. 4). Although kindergarten augments children's past group experiences, there are substantive differences from preschool or child care. Frequently there is less choice of activities and materials. There may be more emphasis on academics and direct instruction. Kindergarten may serve a more diverse population. For the family, contact with the teacher and with the administration is usually more formal (Pianta & Cox).

There are many influences on a child's transition. What are the family expectations? What are the child's social skills? What is the child's economic/cultural/ethnic status? What are the teacher's priorities concerning children's social, behavioral, and academic abilities? Many academic, social, developmental, and communication difficulties are related to poverty and minority status. Adjustment problems are more common in boys and in children from low-income families and families with other risk factors such as "low parent education levels, single parenthood, numerous young siblings, or minority language backgrounds (Zill, 1999, p. 101).

Anecdotes from a survey of 216 kindergarten children and their parents indicated a smooth transition, with children excited about going to "real" school. Negative responses were related to a child having behavioral or emotional difficulties, the schedule having a negative impact on the family, a parent who was nervous about the transition, or a child refusing to go to school (Pianta & Kraft-Sayre, 1999).

Whether the transition is smooth or bumpy, communication between teachers and families seems to make a difference. A study of 110 children in two preschool programs found that a significant source of support came from building partnerships between the schools and kindergarten teachers, and the child, the family, the preschools, and preschool teachers. Preschool visits to kindergartens in the spring, in addition to kindergarten orientation for children and families, was a successful bridging practice (Meier & Schafran, 1999; Pianta, Kraft-Sayre, Rimm-Kaufman, Gercke, & Higgins, 2001). To ease kindergarten jitters in one community, the joint effort of the school and several community organizations resulted in parents accompanying children on their initial bus ride to and from kindergarten in an annual First Riders Program. The actual ride was preceded by a video on bus safety, and a plastic bracelet for each bus child containing name, address, and phone number (Lubell, 2001, p. 4).

A key to transition success seems to be the principal who is able to form liaisons to groups such as preschools, Head Starts, and early intervention programs. An administrator who can "champion home-school connections" sets the tone for a positive kindergarten adjustment (Smolkin, 1999, p. 331).

Entry into early care and education and separation from family provide a ripe opportunity for growth. Self-confidence arises from separations that are well achieved. Children who are supported by their families and teachers as they separate from home have the opportunity to move fearlessly into new realms of learning, growth, and relationships.

3

Learning from Children's Behavior

WHAT ARE SOME of the clues children give us about their feelings connected with leaving home and entering early care and education? Often "leaving home" is a more powerful experience than "entering care or school." Separation events usually involve a slipping back or a giving up in order to step forward. When learning to walk, babies eventually give up crawling. When graduating from high school, teenagers give up the security of known teachers and friends to strike out on their own to college or into the work world. When leaving preschool or child care for kindergarten, 5-year-olds leave a familiar setting. On entering group care, infants and toddlers leave the certainty of home and family for the new ways of the center and caregivers. There is little growth without some pain or anxiety. As we step forward to a new level or challenge, we necessarily leave something behind. Without these dips and rises life would be flat, and people would be undeveloped. Yet the younger the individual, the more help he or she needs in moving forward without wounds. Children tell us through their behavior that they need our help, that their feelings are too overwhelming to manage alone. Let us look at some of these behaviors to become aware of their possible meanings.

VERY GOOD BEHAVIOR

Sometimes children are very good in the classroom. No one can tell they are hurting inside. They keep to themselves. They never get into trouble. Teachers often overlook them in the midst of the swirling life of the classroom. Such a child was Kelly.

Kelly was a 4-year-old boy. His face often wore a blank expression. He rarely smiled. He never cried. He spoke very little. When the group had a music and singing time, Kelly stood at the edge of the seated group, watching. When the group sat for juice and crackers, Kelly sat but refused to eat. When his mother brought him to school, and when she came to pick him up, he was compliant and obedient. He never made a fuss.

Kelly hardly played with any of the equipment. If he painted, it was a lackadaisical three or four strokes of the brush and he was done. He seldom spoke to other children and only spoke to the teacher when asked a direct question. He spoke in short phrases or single words.

When, by November, Kelly's behavior had not changed, the teacher became concerned. She had one clue. Since this was a cooperative nursery school, mothers periodically helped in the room. When Kelly's mother came to help, the teacher noticed a dramatic difference in Kelly's behavior. He was talkative, he ate lustily, he used the equipment, and he seemed to get pleasure in his play.

The teacher arranged a conference with his mother to discuss her concern for the vast difference in Kelly's behavior with and without his mother. They came to the conclusion that perhaps Kelly was missing his mother. It seemed to the teacher that while Kelly was physically in school, he remained mentally at home.

Together, they made plans as if Kelly were again starting school from the first day. His mother began to stay in the room with him for about 1 hour each day. They talked about his missing her. They played together. They planned for her to stay each day that week until snack time. After that first week Kelly and his mother decided together that she would stay once a week. She did so for a month.

At the same time his mother was in the room, Kelly began to relate to the assistant teacher, staying close to her, speaking softly to her. She discovered that if she sat next to him at snack time, he would wait until all the children had left the table and then would eat. He still refused to participate in music time, so the assistant sat next to him, while he stood watching the group. She read to him, led him to the table, and encouraged him to play with dough while she sat next to him. He began to talk more, to both children and adults. He began to use the play equipment. His body relaxed and his face began to exhibit more variety of expressions. By March he had begun to eat when the others ate. By April he began to make a friend, and after spring vacation, he sat near the music group. One day, with the assistant's hand holding his, he took a turn walking around in a circle to the music, wearing his cowboy hat.

He had finally come to preschool.

It was fortunate that Kelly's teacher recognized his lack of involvement in school activities as a separation reaction, even though it was November. By allowing him the time he needed to coalesce his home self with his school self, his teacher and his mother helped him to grow in competence and in self-confidence.

It was also an advantage that his mother was a nurse and that her working hours permitted her to be with Kelly when he came to school in the morning. Another parent, with more conventional working hours, might have been able to stay at the end of the school day, or arrange to come for lunch. Perhaps phoning at strategic times might have helped.

Sometimes, however, children are not at all ready to enter group life. If, for example, Kelly had not made a relationship first with the assistant teacher and then with the children, if he had not started to play, if his body and facial expressions had not relaxed, if he had not started to eat, then he

What may be some of the reasons that a child sits at the edge of an activity?

might have been telling adults that he was not ready to leave home, not ready to come to school. While such situations do not happen frequently, they do occur. Teachers and parents need to be aware of such a possibility and to think about such questions as

- How can a teacher help parents understand that their child is not a failure? How will you work together to help a child understand this?
- How will a connection be maintained between the family and the program so that the child can try again?
- What will a teacher do to alleviate the anxieties of other children in the group who might worry that they, too, might not be ready?
- What will a teacher say to the other parents who might ask, "What happened to that boy? Why isn't he here anymore?"

DELAYED REACTION

Often children do not send out the strong cues that Kelly did. They may come to school bright and bouncy, delighted to be there, excited to play, full of fun and pleasure.

Three-year-old Tania cheerfully kissed her mother goodbye every morning. She painted with enthusiasm, used many colors, and seemed to enjoy her activity. She used dough and water with pleasure and found companionship in the dress-up area. She loved music and books and puzzles. She was a happy-go-lucky girl.

One day, 3 weeks after the program began, she threw herself on the floor, crying hysterically for her mother. She was inconsolable. The teacher phoned her mother that evening to ask if anything unusual had happened. The mother could think of nothing. After all, she recalled, the move to this present new home had taken place several months before.

After that, Tania cried repeatedly when her mother brought her to the center. Together the teacher and the mother decided to see if it would help if the mother stayed a little longer each morning rather than leaving right away. It took several months of this maternal support before Tania felt safe. Even so, Tania occasionally cried for her mother and refused to play.

The move to the new home seemed to be a bigger event in the life of this small girl than anyone had realized. It had taken many months for the child to internalize that experience. It was not until she had been in the center for a few weeks that she was able to express her great distress. Two separations, one from her old home and one from her mother, were more than she could bear.

Children do not have the experience with loss that adults have. They do not know that there are boundaries to these experiences. Children often feel that the loss will never end, that they will never stop feeling sad, that they will never stop crying. They need help to understand that life is not all like this and that the lonely, sad times have ends as well as beginnings. Tania's teacher and her mother, working together toward a common goal— Tania's comfort and ability to control her life—helped her to grow toward the belief that she was a strong person who could overcome hard-to-bear feelings. Tania also learned that though these feelings continued to overwhelm her at times, she could count on her teacher to comfort and support her.

Although young infants up to age 6, 7, or 8 months do not usually display active separation reactions, this may change in the latter part of the first year, as explained in Chapter 2. A vigorous crying protest from a baby may catch a parent off guard, especially since it is most often the parent for whom the separation is the hardest.

REGRESSIVE BEHAVIORS:
THUMB SUCKING, EATING, WETTING, SLEEPING

Three-year-old Tania, discussed above, regressed in her behavior, slipping back to a stage of development that was reminiscent of the toddler. Rex Speers, a psychoanalyst, found that children entering preschool normally repeat phases of their earlier development (Speers, McFarland, Arnaud, & Curry, 1971). He states that this repetition is desirable for children's successful adaptation to school. As they behave in ways that echo their past, Speers writes, children make use of their parents' presence in the classroom to gain self-assurance. Such normal regressions occur when children cry, complain, plead to be taken home, refuse to play, and cling to their parents tenaciously.

Sometimes children need to fall back a few steps in order to move ahead. Perhaps you have noticed that tendency in yourself or in other adults. I once knew a writer who, before he could get down to the serious business of writing, spent half an hour or more checking his various e-mail boxes. It was a bit of avoidant behavior that seemed to provide the needed energy for the task before him.

One of the most obvious remnants of much younger behavior in preschoolers is thumb sucking. Some children who had given it up may, with

In entering preschool, children may interact with their parents as they did when they were toddlers.

the onset of school or child care, begin again, only to give it up once more after they become comfortable. Others who still need to suck their thumbs might be seen sucking more frequently, especially when their parent leaves, at transition times, or when they eat or sleep. It is not uncommon to see children increase their thumb sucking at the end of the day, when they are tired. Some children might also want to return to the comfort of a bottle, even though they had stopped using one. They might need to bring their bottles to school to use for comfort in times of stress.

Do you feel uncomfortable seeing these behaviors? Do you know why? Teachers may worry that if one child has a bottle, or sucks her thumb, that all the children will want bottles or their thumbs. Parents may share these concerns. It is highly unlikely that this will occur, however. Children behave in certain ways because of some specific need. If other children do "copy" them, they will only do it for a short time unless they, too, have a similar need.

Can you observe a child and decide what it means to him to suck his thumb or bottle? Is it important to him? Does it comfort him? Does he engage in other activities in the room besides sucking? When does he stop sucking? How can you as a teacher provide him with more of the times when he does not suck?

You may notice that when he is engaged in activities such as water play, clay, painting, or blocks, he is not inclined to rely on his thumb. A cooking experience or a collage project may offer him worthy substitutes for the self-stimulation of his thumb. In general, children feel better, like adults, when they are productive.

Another regressive behavior related to sucking is seen in eating. The 3-year-old in the following anecdote becomes troubled about his snack.

> Although Sean was busy with blocks, he noticed the teacher handling grapes for snack. He stood up quickly, dropping the block, and cried softly as he rushed over to the teacher, saying, "No, I don't want this, I only want crackers for snack." He spoke quickly, with much feeling.
>
> "Come and look at the food, Sean," said the teacher gently. "These are grapes, and this is cheese. You don't have to eat them, but just come closer and look."
>
> "I don't have to eat them," he whimpered.

Children often display feelings of stress at snack or lunch time. They may eat too little or too much. It's not unusual for toddlers to refuse to eat at all, even though they bring their lunch from home. Food is frequently a tangible reminder of home, and young children may act in a worried manner about eating.

Regression is sometimes seen in children's physical movements. In a study by Curry and Tittnich (1972), children who were "graceful and skillful in performing motor feats" at school entry "suddenly [became] quite clumsy, tripping over nothing at all and causing all sorts of accidents to [themselves] and others" (p. 13).

> Ellie was swaggering in large circles around the room attending to the children and their activity rather than where she was walking. She focused on the children to the front, side, or back, but not on those directly next to her. As a result she tripped and fell three times over children and toys that were in her path. As she fell, she glanced at the obstacle, then immediately regained her far-sighted vision. Her movements were quick as she scrambled to her feet, arms straight, with the palms of her hands flat on the floor to balance herself, as a toddler might.

Toilet accidents and sleep disturbances, especially among 2-and-a-half- and 3-year-olds and sometimes even among 4- and 5-year-olds, are generally common in stressful situations. These regressions of well-learned skills frequently happen around the time children begin early care and education. Parents may notice bed-wetting, constipation, stomachaches, or wet

Enjoyment of eating is often a good clue to comfort.

underpants and clothing. Children may resist going to sleep at school as well as at home. Nap or rest time may find children fidgety, squirming, tense, or unable to stop talking or giggling. Parents may report children waking in the middle of the night, having nightmares, or refusing to go to bed. The opposite may also occur—children who never napped begin to need one, or regular nappers take very long, extended 2- or 3-hour naps.

How many adults, faced with a trip across the country or abroad, moving to a new home, going to college, or starting a new job, find themselves plagued with constipation, diarrhea, loss of appetite, overeating, or sleeplessness? Our bodies often express our feelings, even if we are not aware of them. Children and adults are much alike in this regard.

Nicholas, 26 months old, took a daily afternoon nap at home. When he started child care, he refused to sleep. No amount of rocking, back rubbing, singing, or vocal soothing would induce him to sleep. Finally the caregiver stopped trying to give him a nap and allowed him to play after lunch instead. Often he fell asleep on a soft chair or couch. After a few weeks of this he allowed the caregiver to put him on a cot in the nap room.

One-year-old Mara finished her bottle sitting on her caregiver's lap. When the caregiver put her on her cot, she lay down for a second. Then she popped up, saying "lights," "Hi," "children." "Yes, the lights are out. It's nap time," the caregiver says. Finally, after 5 minutes of Mara popping up and down on the cot, the caregiver picks her up, wraps a blanket around her, rocks her in the rocking chair, sings quietly to her, and in moments, Mara is asleep. The caregiver puts her on her cot and covers her.

Why might young children be so worried about sleeping at naptime? In falling asleep, children give up whatever small amount of control they have over themselves when they are awake. Giving it up, for some children, is not easily done. It is especially difficult at a time when they are worried about where their parents are and whether or not their parents will know where to find them. Some children think that if they are not sure where their parents are, then their parents may not be sure where they, their children, are.

While regressions in motor control, eating, toileting, sleeping, and sucking are frequently associated with separation reactions, they are also commonly seen whenever children feel stress, either at home or at school.

LOOKING AND TALKING

Often children show through looking and talking that they are not yet able to rely on an inner image of their parent as a source of comfort and reassurance. They require an extra dose of teacher and parental help.

Two-and-a-half-year-old Christopher needed his grandmother to sit in the room with him for more than a week before she was able to move to a small library room connected to the classroom. Christopher often walked into the room and circled around her. When he

The parent can be seen sitting nearby. The distance between parent and child is distinct yet minimal, fostering the boy's developing capacity for trust.

was in the classroom, he frequently looked in through the open door, checking to see if she were still there.

A child's internal picture comes from repeated interactions and experiences with the loved person. The ability to hold this image develops slowly and in toddlers is unstable when the person is away. Christopher used his eyes as well as language as techniques to maintain his grandmother's image.

> "I will not cry," he said. "No, I will not cry. Nana will not go? No, Nana will not go. She will be in the library. She will not leave Christopher. Christopher will go to school. Nana will wait in the library."
> Despite the grandmother's repeated reassurances that she would wait in the library, he asked the same questions again and again.

Children's use of language may provide other clues to their feelings about separation. Refusal to talk, reversion to baby talk, or excessive talking may be signals that a child is worried.

Four-year-old Shawnique never spoke a word to the teacher during the entire year. She spoke only occasionally to other children although she played frequently with them. She used materials, listened to stories, and sat on the teacher's lap but she refused to speak to her despite the teacher's most creative efforts. Her mother said that she never stopped talking at home.

This girl's refusal to speak possibly indicated her incomplete separation adaptation. Perhaps it was her way of leaving a part of herself at home.

While some children may display anxiety through silence or continual talking, others may use language to master their feelings. A teacher's or parent's words, too, can help, even with the youngest children. However, "Mom will be back right after lunch (or nap)" is reassuring only if it is true.

Sometimes children use words to reassure themselves, as if the words themselves had a physical presence.

Every morning, Miriam looked at her mother and questioned, "Are you going to work? At the hospital?"

"Yes," her mother replied while kissing and hugging her. "Bye-bye! Have a nice time today."

Miriam took the teacher's proffered hand, saying, "My mommy is going to work. To the hospital. I'll stay in school. She'll come back to get me, right?" The teacher reassured her that her mother would be back after work. Miriam went to paint at the easel.

Through their language, children have the ability to let someone know that they need help.

Jacob, in the midst of snack time, begins to sob. "I want my mama!" Three other children watch him intently. The teacher hugs him and says, "I guess you're missing your mama. She'll be coming back soon." He stops crying and reorganizes himself. The other children seem visibly relieved.

Michael (2-and-a-half years old) is finishing his breakfast, when across the room, Susan's mother is getting ready to leave. Michael frowns and calls out to the caregiver, "Susan's mommy reminds me of my mommy." He scrunches up his face and is about to cry. "Sometimes other people's mommies remind us of saying goodbye to our own mommies." "Yeah," he says, "my mommy went to work already. But she'll be back after nap."

Language, however fledgling, can help even a very young child become master of the coming and going.

> One-year-old Ava watches her mother leave. "Out!" she says. Later, when her mother returns, she smiles, rushes to her arms, and says, "Back!"

Children's language offers other opportunities for a teacher to take some appropriate action. In a music session with 4-year-olds, reported in a preschool teacher's log, children share their feelings with the teacher, who is later able to sing songs about mothers and encourage children to move to music, permitting them to dramatize their feelings of missing their mothers.

> As we were about to start music, Demian buried his face in his hands and burst into tears. "I miss my mom!" he cried bitterly. I noticed several other children start to cry. Their faces seemed to say the same thing: "I miss my mom!"
>
> This was not unprecedented. We had been having a rash of children missing their mothers over the past few weeks, but nothing as blatant as this. For this reason, I had made a family scrapbook. Children had brought in pictures of their families and could look at them in times of need.
>
> When I asked the children if they missed their moms, they all, with definite feeling, said they did. As I began playing a soft song, everyone, with the sole exception of Norman, got up and started dancing. The children moved gracefully, feelingly to the music. There was a sharing of this "I miss you" emotion. Norman sat on the sidelines, observing wistfully.
>
> (Small, 1983, p. 31)

Coping with separation may take the form of using baby talk instead of more mature language. Help children by acknowledging this regression as a normal step in growing up. Admonishing them to speak in their normal manner often makes them feel ashamed for having shared their secret longings with you. In the following anecdote, the teacher who used music responds to baby talk in his 4-year-old group.

> As the group settles down for music, I noticed Eleanor and Amy engaged in "ga ga" talk. I saw a dazzling array of different feelings expressed through playful body language and cooing tones. I had the feeling that they were completely themselves. Vanished for the

moment were the pretenses and obfuscations of feelings so often accompanying the use of proper language.

Sensing the moment ripe for baby movement, I asked, "Show me how you move like a baby." Silence. Shocked, blank faces. The children momentarily became stupefied when confronted with the reality of acting out some of their repressed fantasies.

Finally, after a long silence, Adam volunteered. He is strong, secure, and playfully rebellious—far removed from a helpless "baby self." He was in a position to venture into the "baby" role and have fun with it.

And what fun he had! Getting on hands and knees, he playfully crawled, rolled, and scampered around the floor. All the while he made playful, realistic baby sounds. Soon all the others followed.

(Small, 1983, p. 25)

INCREASED DEPENDENCE

Perhaps, as a teacher, you have seen otherwise competent children become increasingly dependent during the program's first weeks. They refuse to dress themselves or protest that they cannot, demand help in the simplest of tasks, refuse to pour their own juice or milk, need your lap many times during the day, and cling, follow, or shadow you or other adults in the room. These behaviors seem to say, "I am feeling very little and not up to my usual competent self. Give me just a little extra babying for a short period of time, and it will provide the fuel I need so that I can get up and go on my own steam."

Parents may notice similar behaviors at home. For example, Khallel wants to be dressed in the morning; Jason refuses to be dressed. Camillo constantly crawls into his mother's lap; Sophie follows her mother from room to room, crying if she goes out of view. Parents and teachers will suspect that these are beginning-school behaviors. They are, for the most part, temporary and will probably disappear as a child is reassured that she has been sent to early education and care to have a good, happy time and that the teachers can take care of her. Trust of this sort takes time to develop.

Have you ever noticed that many behaviors associated with eating, sleeping, competence, language, and toileting are exhibited again by children when they return to the program after an illness or an extended absence? Have you noticed children behaving in some of these ways when strangers enter the room for a visit? Or when the familiar room arrangement is changed? There seem to be common elements in these situations.

SECURITY OBJECTS

Remember Linus and his blanket in the *Peanuts* cartoon? We laugh at Linus because so many children bring shreds of blankets, tattered and rubbed-out stuffed animals, old diapers, or other "cozys" to early care or school with them. Perhaps you remember having such a security object yourself. Somehow these things seem to make children feel safe, as though they have brought a bit of home with them.

Children seem to grant special qualities to security objects and endow them with important powers. Just watch what happens when a child misplaces his object and cannot find it! Or see how toddlers spontaneously bring the correct favorite cozy to comfort a crying baby. A well-known psychiatrist, D. W. Winnicott (1957), calls these "transitional objects." He explains: "It is not the object itself, of course, that is transitional; it represents the infant's transition from a state of being merged with the mother to a state of being in relation to the mother as something outside and separate" (p. 183).

Where she goes, there goes her blanket.

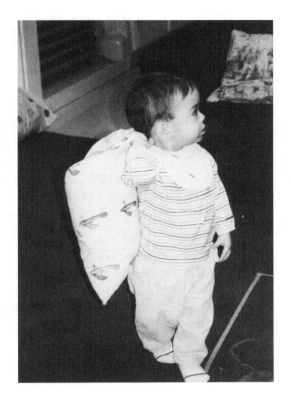

A stuffed animal isn't always the security object of choice. In this case, his pillow assures him of home and family.

The teddy bear or blanket supports children's journey to growing up from infancy to early childhood. This journey leads them away from being part of the parent toward being persons separate from the parent. Because these objects have such significance for young children, they seem to provide a sense of security when children move from the familiarity of the home to the unfamiliarity of the school or center. The objects children bring from home are often more important than the activities to which they are drawn in school:

> Ilana worked with pegs and puzzles while holding on to a ring that was far too large for her to wear on her finger. She would not let go of it even though it made using the manipulative toys she was working with more difficult.
>
> (Paul, 1975, p. 40)

In one situation, a 2-year-old child used an experience with his father as his transitional object. The father came crawling into the classroom with the child on his back. Both were growling. After the father left, the child continued to growl for a period of time during the morning and at isolated times during the day.

Sometimes children use things from the classroom itself as transitional objects in an effort to master their separation feelings.

> Daniella strode over to the dress-up shelf. She began to throw clothes and shoes haphazardly over her shoulder, tossing them into the air, until she found her favorite black derby hat. She popped it on her head. A large grin immediately appeared on her face.
>
> Several times during the day she was seen looking at herself in the mirror while wearing the derby. For months she frequently wore it all morning, even putting it under her cot when she took a nap.

Many babies and toddlers rely on pacifiers even when the urgent sucking needs of the earliest months of life are past.

> Gideon, 19 months, is in the yard rolling a ball when the group gathers to go indoors for lunch. Transitions like this are often hard for him. He stops suddenly, looks at the teacher, and wails "Mama." "Mommy will come back, mommy always comes back," she reassures him and gives him his *three* pacifiers. He pops one into his mouth and holds one in each hand. He calms and leans against her.

Some children arrive in their center or family child care home with a pacifier pinned to their shirt, available for times of stress or fatigue. It's hard to tell which need is satisfied by a *bo-bo*, the word used by many families. Is it a transitional object, reminder of the parent? Until what age is it necessary? Does it interfere with a child's speech? Nagging questions and opinions surround the use of pacifiers.

For infants and toddlers, however, the caregiver him- or herself is their most important transitional object, aside from the parent. This makes an open-and-shut case for primary caregiving as illustrated in the following anecdote.

> It is late afternoon in the Baby Room. It is Zelda's first week at [the center] without her parents. She is just three months old. She is lying on her back under a kind of baby mobile blanket. She seems quite content just looking around. Every so often her fist goes past her eyes and she appears to really notice and to the best of her

ability seems to hold it in place so she can continue to look at it. Sitting next to her is her primary caregiver, who notices Zelda's accomplishment and comments on it. The caregiver's voice seems to take pride in the baby's ability. Suddenly Zelda goes from being content to being totally discontent. Her cry is loud and painful and piercing. The caregiver gently picks her up and holds her close. She walks back and forth with her for what seems an eternity. Her voice is calming and she gently rocks her, saying over and over "sh sh sh sh sh." Zelda quiets and her caregiver continues the slow and gentle movement for a while longer.

(P. Sradnick, from student journal, 2002)

Resch states that, "Gratifying care is that which surrounds the basics of feeding, diapering and putting to sleep with fondling, handling, cooing, babbling, talking and playing." These routines are "major and rich sources of gratification . . . [providing] the confident expectation, and the real experience, of a continuity of gratifying care" that helps infants develop the capacity to separate from their parents (Resch, 1977, p. 261).

Since children also turn to their security objects and persons during transitions in the day's schedule or at times when the curriculum activity ends or breaks down, teachers will need to distinguish between those situations, heightened other stress, and separation reactions.

RELATIONS WITH OTHER CHILDREN

Through their uncomfortable relations with other children and with adults, young children often show that separation is more stressful than they can handle. This may take the form of belligerence or withdrawal. Do not assume that all angry behavior is connected to separation reactions, however.

The same Christopher who worried and clung to his grandmother in the library also provoked others and disobeyed the teacher.

Christopher saw a plastic cauliflower that Joshua had dropped on the floor. When Christopher grabbed it, Joshua, astonished, said, "Hey, that's mine!" Angrily, Christopher threw it in Joshua's face. Joshua yelled, "I don't like that!" and glared at Christopher, who opened his eyes wide, laughed mischievously, and ran off in circles all around the room.

When the teacher told Christopher to pick up the cauliflower and to talk to Joshua about it, Christopher ran to the bookshelf and sat down to look at a book.

Why would children who are feeling worried about separation hit others, be disobedient, or destroy things in the classroom? Consider this: One way to get rid of scary feelings is to fight them by taking very active steps. Throwing things, hitting, or arguing with others gives one the illusion of tremendous activity. It is as if children feel that they must do something to make themselves feel less worried. They are less concerned with the consequences of their antisocial behavior than they are with eliminating the fear they feel.

Sometimes children behave in a frantic manner:

> Adam . . . flitted around from one thing to another. . . . When the teacher tried to get him to [complete] a drawing, he told her . . . "I can't—you do it!" He treated the guinea pig like an inanimate object . . . he ran around the room as if he expected to be chased.
>
> He did not pay any attention to his mother . . . when she left. But when a girl spoke to her father on the play phone, he grabbed the phone out of her hand and said, "When are you coming back?" On a number of occasions he ran in the opposite direction when he was told that it was time to go home and that his mother was waiting for him.
>
> Although he seemed almost desperate to make contact with children, he went about it by repeating what they said, grabbing things from them, taking over what they were doing, and trying to create excitement by getting silly with them.
>
> (Paul, 1975, pp. 36–37)

Behaviors like these can drive adults to clamp down and restore peace. However, doing so shuts out the opportunity to help children reflect on and gain control of their emotions. "I see that you are unhappy and thinking about your daddy, so I will help you find something fun to do." The challenge for adults is how to stop the behavior while at the same time acknowledge with the child his or her underlying feelings.

COPING THROUGH PLAY

It is, perhaps, through play that children find their most satisfactory means of coming to terms with and mastering their reactions to separation. Developing cognitive skills is necessary for children to understand separation (Resch, 1975). Before age 3, a child begins to attach meaning and feelings to a parent's departure. To the extent that he can use a caregiver's presence and eventually language and play to find relief from sad and angry feelings, he shows his potential for growth.

> Three-year-old Marina throws her doll out of her room every morning before going to preschool. She tells her mother, "I don't want to go to school." Her mother acknowledges this by saying, "I know you don't want to go." Then she helps Marina dress, gives her breakfast, and takes her to school. Marina initiates a hide-and-seek game with the teacher when she arrives. This goes on for several months.

What can we say about Marina? Is this a problem or is this a child at work, coping with leaving home and going to school? Marina is using symbolic play to aid her adjustment to this new experience. She is practicing control over her own life. It is she who throws the doll out of the room, unlike the real situation in which she is taken to preschool. In playing hide-and-seek, it is she who has the control, unlike the real situation. In the real situation she has no control, for it is her mother who decides to take her, and leaves her at school.

As adults, we attempt to manage our feelings and behavior when events occur over which we have little control. It is when we lose control, when we are unable to rally ourselves to take action, that we feel unsatisfied with ourselves and defeated. Children feel the same way.

Role-playing is an important and self-initiated activity that serves a multitude of functions. Through roles, children try out various ways of "being." Taking on the role of the one who offers nurturing may be one way a child can be both nurtured as well as nurturing. In tending to a doll, a girl may be caring for the doll as if the doll were herself. In the following anecdote of two 3-year-old boys, the roles of baby and mother are clearly enacted, allowing both children to feel cared for as well as caring.

> Andrew is the mother. At his feet is a wicker laundry basket with Nathan sitting in it. He is the baby. Andrew gives Nathan an affectionate look and asks, "Do you want more?" The "baby" replies in a high, squeaky voice, "Yes." Andrew carefully places himself down into the basket, half resting on the edge. His chest is about on eye level with the "baby." He sticks his chest out, offering his "breast" to the "baby." The "baby" pretends to suck through Andrew's shirt. Andrew wraps his left arm snuggly around the "baby's" neck. He has a very serious look on his face.

The child feels nurtured as well as nurturing.

Play of this sort may help children feel more confident about their parents' continuing nurturance even though they are not present. Witnessing such an intimate scene may cause some adults discomfort. However, it is natural for very young boys to "try out" maternal, as well as paternal, activities in their play.

Make-believe is a rich resource of healing for preschool children. You may see children soothing their own feelings as you observe them at play. You may see them attempting to gain control, as in "fighting fires."

> Gerald was riding a trike and making siren-like sounds. He abruptly jumped off the trike and ran toward the opposite end of the playground, yelling, "Fire! Fire! Quick, there's a fire over there. Get the fire hats, hurry!" He pulled a hat out of the box, plopped it on his head, and rushed back toward his parked trike, shouting "Hurry! The fire! We need to put out the fire! C'mon! Fire! Fire!"

Perhaps the dangerous fire was a symbol for things that often raged out of control in Gerald's small life. Play is one way a child can practice being in charge.

As children begin to adapt to school and to the temporary loss of a parent, they begin to demonstrate their tolerance for "the existence of 'goodness' or 'badness' in [themselves] as well as in [their] mother" (Curry & Tittnich, 1972, p. 28). They play out this theme in different ways. It may involve "good baby-bad baby" games, "good guy-bad guy" roles, or, as in the following anecdote, a girl's being "bad" herself:

> Jessica rushed over to Jamie, quickly grabbed the car from his hand, darted across the room, and hid behind the teacher. When she saw Jamie rushing toward her, yelling "Jamie's car!" Jessica dropped the car and ambled over to the telephone. Picking up the receiver, she shouted, "Bad girl! You are a bad girl! Bad girl! You are such a bad girl!"

This play helped Jessica, who was having difficulty leaving her mother, come to terms with the good as well as the bad in herself. A month after this incident, she became a full-fledged class participant. Though the "bad" behavior resurfaced, it was short-lived. Her entry into preschool was both positive and enthusiastic.

> Jessica swooped into the room, ran over to Jamie, and snatched a small car from his hand. When Jamie protested loudly "No!" and half-rose to his feet, Jessica dropped the car, ran over to her cubby, skillfully unzipped her coat, and hung it on the hook. She rushed over to the shelf, picked up a toy car, plopped down next to Jamie, and pushed her car next to his.

The younger the children, the less able they are to use fully developed play in their attempts to gain mastery over their feelings. Children two and under are more directly imitative than symbolic in their play, yet this form of play gives them a chance to express themselves. Rebecca, 19 months old, had spent most of the day in the center in a happy frame of mind.

> After lunch several children arrived at the center with their parents for the afternoon session. As one after the other of the parents bid goodbye to the children, Rebecca began to cry. She stood near the door, sobbing, repeatedly waving "bye-bye" and throwing kisses.

In reenacting the morning parting from her own parents Rebecca gave vent to feelings that she had been containing. Her expression of such deep emotion drew the caregiver to her, and she accepted the comfort of a lap and a hug.

Play can also take the form of interacting with materials such as blocks, paints, crayons, water, or play dough. Through the creation of something with these materials, children are able to externalize some of their worry about separation. For example, 2- and 3-year-olds often fear masks. They frequently believe that a mask is real and that the person wearing it is, indeed, a wolf, monster, or witch. They are equally afraid of putting on a mask. Perhaps they believe that if they do, they will change identity or that they will disappear. They may believe, when they see an adult put on a mask, that she or he has disappeared and has now become the witch or wolf. Here there are similarities with separation. The younger the children, the less able they are to understand that when a person leaves, he or she does not disappear. So it is with masks. While most 4-year-olds understand that an adult still exists beneath the mask, many 3- and 2-year-olds are just as sure that she does not. Thus, for a 3-year-old, making a mask and being in charge of putting it on and taking it off in front of a mirror may be one way of adding some understanding about the appearance-disappearance aspects of separation.

> Isaac came close to the paper bag masks that the children were making. He seemed frightened and started to run away. He watched intently as the teacher put on a mask. When he looked through the holes in the bag and saw the teacher's face, he laughed. He placed a paper bag over his own head and looked at himself in the mirror. He began to select materials to paste on the bag. He became relaxed and thoughtful. Finished, he sang out, "I made a mask!", patting his chest for emphasis. As another teacher walked by, Isaac shouted with glee, "I made this. I'm gonna scare you!"

Children use the theme of appearance-disappearance in a variety of ways. Peekaboo is an age-old favorite that children begin to play as early as 6 or 7 months of age. In those early months, the game allows the baby to experiment with the permanence of things and people. First you are here, then you are gone, and now you are back again! It is a way of learning that things and people exist even though they are not in sight. Babies play it again and again; learning that there is stability in the world takes a long time.

> Ten-month-old Soraya sits on the floor next to Kate, her caregiver, while she folds laundry. Kate puts a clean cloth over the head of

Soraya, saying "Where's Soraya?" Pulling it off, laughing, Kate says, "There she is!" Soraya laughs, takes the cloth and holds it against her own face. They repeat the game several times. Soraya changes the game by holding the cloth toward Kate's head. Kate puts it over her head, saying, "Where's Kate?" Soraya pulls the cloth off Kate's head and they both laugh gleefully.

> (K. Estrellado, from student journal, 2001)

This game also allows young children to develop the means for coping with separation. In essence, separation is, after all, "You're here, you're gone, and now you're back." Peekaboo is both a rehearsal for and a recapitulation of the separation experience.

There are many variations on the theme of peekaboo. A 2-year-old who wraps and unwraps his play dough with a large sheet of paper is playing the game in his own style. The following anecdote reveals how Jamal, a 2-year-old who had a hard time separating from her mother, plays out some of her feelings with a small covered box containing a toy bear and a tiny blanket.

Jamal cried hard for a long time after her mother left, even while in the enveloping arms of Jonathan, her primary caregiver. When she finally calmed down, her eyes lit on a small box. She opened it and grinned when she saw the tiny bear inside. Removing the bear and the small blanket, she laid them both on the floor. Then she put the bear back in the box. "He's crying," she said as she patted him. The box fell over and the bear rolled out. "Do you want to go to sleep in there?" Putting the bear back in, she said, "I cover him up." She closed the box and carried it as she walked around. Again she put it on the floor, opened it, and took the bear out. Rubbing her fingers over the bear, she put him back in and closed the cover. Opening the cover, she patted the bear three times and said, "G'night."

In comforting the crying bear, Jamal seemed to be reenacting both the feelings she had when she cried as well as the comforting she received from her primary caregiver. In the ritual of opening and closing the box, taking the bear in and out, she may have been reassuring herself that her mother, though gone, would come back. A significant aspect of this play situation is that the child has the upper hand. It is the child who says good-bye, who does the leaving, who controls the appearance and disappearance. This sort of play adds to a child's growing sense of self-reliance.

Is there an adult among us who has not relied on telephone play?

After winter break, James (2.8 years) picks up the wooden phone every day and asks the teacher to call his mother at work. Lori dials the number and says, "Hi, James' mom, it's James' teacher, Lori. James wants to talk to you." She hands the phone to James who takes it with a big smile. "Hi mommy, I miss you. I want you to pick me up. I'll see you later." He hangs up and tells Lori, "She said she's coming to pick me up!"

Geronimo (20 months) picks up a small telephone and says "Hello? Hello?" Maria, his primary caregiver says, "Who is it? Geronimo are you calling mommy?" He says "Hello. Hello. Mommy," and hands the phone to Maria. "Hi Geronimo's mommy. She wants to talk to you again." Geronimo takes the phone. "Hello? Hello. Mommy."

Children accept the telephone, even though it is not real, because it seems to provide a most tangible and concrete link to their absent parent.

WHEN PARENTS RETURN

We have been focusing our attention on children when they are left by their parents. However, we must not neglect the reunion of parents and children at the end of the class session or at the end of the day. What happens then is often revealing and frequently misunderstood.

Have you ever had an experience like this? A parent comes to call for her son, expecting a warm and loving greeting at the end of the day. No such thing happens! The boy refuses to leave, runs around the room, begins to paint or takes blocks off the shelf, tries to put on dress-up clothes, or insists that the teachers now need his help in cleaning up the room. The parent begins to become annoyed and is forced to insist that the boy come home. He goes reluctantly.

On the other hand, a child may cry when a parent comes, may refuse to speak, or may turn away from parental attempts at a hug or kiss.

What could be operating here? You might think that the child likes the center better than home or the teacher more than the parent. While that may be true at some moments, it is not true in the majority of cases.

All during the day, children have been actively managing their angry or sad feelings about being left. When the end of the day comes, they find it hard to maintain that coping stance, and they may break down. Crying shows that they have reached their limit of dealing with these feelings.

Refusal to go home, giving a parent a hard time, and acting as if they do not wish to greet parents in a loving way are all behaviors that say, in effect, "You left me here this morning. Now it's my chance to leave you by staying here. Now I can give you a dose of what you gave me this morning." Lieberman (1993) states that

> reunions deserve as much attention and care as separations . . . A reunion is colored by the emotional baggage of the separation experience, and some ambivalence is inevitably attached to it . . . It takes some time to process the reality of the separation, to let go of the coping mechanisms one used for dealing with it, and to relax into being together again. (pp. 215–216)

While in most cases, a child's avoidance of parents at reunion time is normal, there are some cases in which a teacher may want to take a closer look. If a child consistently ignores or rejects his or her parents, in the mornings as well as the evenings, this may indicate a problem in the parent-child relationship. A small percentage of the children in the studies done by Ainsworth (Ainsworth & Wittig, 1969) refused to respond to their mothers at reunion, ignored them, or rejected their attempts at greeting. Because of the persistence of this phenomenon, she labeled such children as ambivalent in their feelings toward their mothers or as "insecurely attached." If you as a teacher have concerns about a particular parent-child pair, consider having a conference with the parent(s). If you feel that the problem is beyond your competence, share this with the parent(s). You may both decide that seeking help from a child guidance center or a child psychologist is warranted.

It is not unusual for teachers to interpret children's rejecting-of-parents behavior as an indication of their own superior ability to form a relationship with the child. This leads to competition with the parents, which is never helpful to child or parent.

Most children are delighted to see their parents at the end of the day.

> Eighteen-month-old Kayla stood at the window, intently watching for her mother's return. When she caught sight of her mother, she danced up and down and called "Mama!" The mother came close to the window, smiled broadly, saying "Hi!" and waving. When she disappeared briefly as she made her way to the door, Kayla cried and called for her. Kayla was relieved to see her reappear several seconds later and fell into her arms. Each day she repeats this ritual. It is becoming easier for her to wait for the reunion that happens after the mother's brief disappearance.

OTHER SEPARATION REACTIONS

Separation reactions do not always go away after children have happily settled in the classroom. Teachers and parents may be surprised to see some of the old behaviors appearing in related situations. Perhaps you teach a group of 4-year-olds. As children begin to have their 5th birthdays, you may notice an increased anxiety in some who begin to talk about kindergarten. Many 4-year-olds believe that on the day they become 5 they will go to kindergarten. They begin to suffer the separation blues until they understand that they will not have to leave the security of their present preschool immediately.

Feelings about separation may erupt in situations that remind children of their original separation experience. As noted earlier, a resurgence of clinginess or a renewal of crying may occur when children return to a program after an illness or a vacation. It is as though they were going through a shortened version of their first entry. There may also be a revival of these reactions when the teacher returns to the classroom after having been away for a time. It is not unusual for children to express angry feelings toward their teacher for being away from the classroom for a few days, no matter the reason for the absence. Separation reactions may also appear on Mondays when children leave home after the weekend or on Fridays when children leave school or group care.

A teacher's reaction to children will be important. Accepting these feelings with understanding aids a child's knowledge that certain emotions are appropriate. Such understanding will also help parents who may be mystified by their children's behavior in these circumstances.

Similar reactions are frequently seen at the end of the term. Children are not very ceremonious about saying goodbye at that time. Many teachers feel let down when children blithely skip out the door without so much as a backward glance. One teacher I know found herself in tears as the last child nonchalantly left the room. Often young children cannot comprehend that they will not be coming back the following week.

Some children do feel the pain of parting on the final day but do not know how to express it. The following record of a child's last day is a good example of the mixed feelings of anger and sadness that many of us, children and adults, feel when an important event draws to a close.

> At the final day family picnic, Janine passes by the two teachers who are seated on a blanket. She shoots a quick glance at them and runs to her father.
>
> She returns in a few minutes with a ball and starts to play—still not too close. Although the teachers speak to her, she does not look

at them. When they ask her to sit with them, she gives them a hostile stare.

Abruptly she runs across the grass to a table where slices of watermelon are available. Gazing wistfully at her teachers from that distance, she eats her watermelon. Slowly she approaches, again appearing nonchalant, pointedly not responding to their remarks. She refuses to join them on their blanket, but sits on the grass, her back to them. Suddenly she turns and says, over her shoulder, "Hey, I'm scrapin' this watermelon like an artichoke!" Showing the teachers the rind, she scrapes it with her teeth. Then, just as suddenly, her face becomes downcast and she crawls up between the two teachers and, touching both, curls up and puts her thumb in her mouth.

HOW OBSERVATIONS CAN HELP

Teachers' own keen observations of children's behavior are a most fruitful source of knowledge. Taking brief anecdotal records of the child with the parent on their first day, or during the first week, may provide a rich resource for both helping the child and conferring with a parent if the need arises. Be alert to the possibility of your own bias warping the actual observed behavior. There is a world of difference between the two following brief anecdotes of the same incident. In which one does the teacher's bias come through?

Cindy sat in her mother's lap during the entire morning session. Her body was rigid and she frequently covered her eyes with her hands. Her mother cradled Cindy in her arms. She made no attempt to interest Cindy in any of the activities.

Cindy is a really spoiled child. Her mother is no help at all, holding Cindy close to her on her lap. Cindy doesn't even try to play with anything.

It is not unusual for teachers' opinions or expectations of how children should behave to interfere with their "seeing" what is happening. Taking records of children as they arrive with their parents, as well as when they leave with their parents, may provide a closeup of the separation process. If such records are taken over a 2-month period, at 2- or 3-week intervals, a teacher may be able to identify patterns of separation for individual children. Observing and recording behavior associated with separation will increase awareness and aid in daily planning with parents for those children whose separation is not smooth. (For further information, see Cohen, Stern, & Balaban, 1997.)

Becoming aware of the ways in which young children communicate their concerns about leaving their parents puts both teacher and parents in a firm position to help them. Coping with stress and gaining mastery over feelings are important requisites for maturing. Assuming that children will "get over it" or "grow out of it" does not provide them with the opportunity to work through their feelings. In an environment of understanding and support, children become competent and self-confident. They learn not only how to leave, but how to venture out—how to try new things.

When you, as a teacher, say, "Sure you can sit on my lap. I know how you feel. You must be missing your mom," you are helping a child understand that his feelings of loneliness and grief are both legitimate and ac-

The teacher can do the most for children when they enter the classroom for the first time. Her support and caring helps children grow toward indpendence.

ceptable. You can help him cope with those feelings through your friendship. As a teacher or parent, you can help children understand that their feelings have an end as well as a beginning. You can help them master their feelings by putting those feelings into words. You can help them know that you have confidence that they are persons who can cope with those feelings, can receive help from another human being, and can then go on to act in an age-appropriate way with pleasure. They are on their way, with your help, to becoming sturdy and happy young children able to function successfully without their parents in a safe, nurturing, and trustful environment. Working together, teachers and parents have provided them with this possibility for growth and with the potential for coping successfully with many future separations.

4

Using Curriculum to Cope with Separation

IN CHAPTER 3 WE looked at behaviors that provide clues to children's feelings as they enter early care and education. We also considered some ways that children cope with their fears and tensions about separation.

What can be done to encourage children's attempts at coping so that they emerge from their early education separation experiences as strong, capable, and self-reliant individuals? How can the curriculum of an early care and education program be used to fortify these children? Although the focus of this chapter is on the teacher and curriculum development, parents can engage their children at home in many of the activities described below in order to support them in coping with separation reactions.

Curriculum begins with you, the teacher. It is based on what you know about the developmental abilities, interests, and needs of each child in your group. Curriculum for young children is what happens between you and the children, between the children themselves, and between the children and the activities, events, and materials you have chosen to provide.

Curriculum is not merely a series of lesson plans or "recipes" that tell you what to do in each situation that arises in the classroom life. Water play, for example, cannot be described as effective curriculum apart from you, the teacher. As curriculum it depends on how you set it up, how you understand its value, how you mediate between the children and the uses they make of the water, and what your reasons are for offering it to the children. If you stand near the water play area, mopping up every spill, admonishing children to be careful, or directing children in how to use it, you are providing one kind of curriculum. If you allow the children to explore the water freely in their own ways, perhaps covering the table that holds

The teacher's involvement with children in water play builds strong bonds.

the water basins with toweling to minimize spills and encouraging them to clean up themselves, you are providing a very different kind of curriculum, certainly a different experience for the children.

The topic of separation is as viable an aspect of early childhood curriculum as is water play, and similar thinking applies. The use you make of separation as curriculum will depend on what you believe about separation and how you choose to use it in the day-to-day life of your classroom. Curriculum, according to Greenman (1988), "is responding to the persistent ache of separation that at times resonates throughout a room of babies like a melancholy foghorn . . . Care and learning together are the curriculum" (p. 48). The caregiver in the following examples, carries forward her curriculum goal of easing separation stress by acknowledging the mother's and then the child's feelings.

Kim is saying goodbye to her 8-month-old daughter who is in the arms of her primary caregiver, Joan. Kim looks pained when the baby cries. She starts to go several times, returning with each cry to kiss the baby again. Finally, with tears filling her eyes, she leaves. Later that morning Joan phones Kim at work to tell her that the baby "cried a little, then stopped, and now she's OK." Kim gave an audible sigh of relief. "Thanks for calling."

Later Joan makes another curriculum decision. She leads weepy 3-year-old, Sebastian, whose father has just left, to the sand table where she hides two small cars and says, "Goodbye!" Sebastian digs them out; Joan says "Hello!" and buries them again. After a few minutes of playing hide-and-seek with cars and sand, he relaxes, smiles, and leans against her affectionately.

Think of separation as a curriculum *process* rather than as a single event. Imagine curriculum as a necklace with several strands of beads. One of those strands is called "separation." It stretches from the beginning of the school year to the end and is dotted with beads representing different activities. However, no one bead alone makes up the strand, as no one strand makes up the necklace. As you begin to provide children with activities to alleviate their separation stress, you will be providing them with your knowledge of the psychological roots of attachment and separation, and your ongoing concern for their positive growth and development. You and the children are the strand upon which the beads are strung.

Let us, at this point, reexamine the characteristics of the separating children described in Chapter 3 in order to reflect on curriculum decisions.

CHILDREN WHO ARE "TOO GOOD"

The important first step is to decide that you want to help "too-good" children. They are often hard to reach because they demand so much time and energy. You have to keep working at your relationship with them. This is admittedly troublesome because there is a class full of children clamoring for you. These quiet "good" children do not always make speedy progress, and it may take many weeks of reassurance and your continuing attention until they are able to function on their own. It may also necessitate parent contact, which is described in Chapter 5.

These children often need interchanges with you alone before they are able to relate to other children. Stories read while the child sits on your lap, games played with you, and clean-up chores done together are opportunities for intimate contact that build a trusting relationship.

The following excerpts from a teacher's 2-month observational log give a close view of her work with one of these "good" children—3-year-old Diana.

11/10 Diana seems to love the affectionate attention of other children, but she is not yet ready to interact with them. She does not seem to have a strong voice of her own yet. Her sparse language and her tentative steps toward involvement may indicate that Diana does not feel entirely comfortable about classroom life.

11/13 Diana still seems not quite in school. She has a faraway expression and roams around, touching a puzzle, a book, but can't seem to settle anywhere. "Would you like to do something with me?" I ask. She looks pleased and shakes her head "yes." We choose a stacking toy. She climbs on my lap, nuzzles into my arms, leans against me, puts her hand on my knees, and I hear her breathe deeply.

11/20 Diana is using puppets, singing a song that comes from deep inside her, "La la la la." They are a very useful prop to get Diana out of her withdrawn state. She is really able to show a wide range of feelings, and the puppets have helped her get on with her language development.

It also seems as if the verbal interaction and the affectionate demonstration with momma and baby puppet helped Diana to deal with her separation feelings. She brought momma into the classroom when she needed her. A giant step for Diana.

11/26 Diana was very engrossed, using crayons and paper. "Look" she said, "I made a girl." It was indeed a representation: The first she had done in school.

Later she began to tie her shoe. After much effort and concentration, she got the two loops together. Excitedly she flew over to me. "I tied my shoes myself!"

The two incidents, so close to each other, are further proof of Diana's growth.

12/11 I thought it would help finalize their separation if Diana could watch her mom go out the door each morning and then wave to her, on the street below, from the window. This kind of sequencing seems to help Diana. It gave her a certain amount of control over the separation, rather than merely *being* left.

12/15 Today is Monday—sometimes hard to say good-bye. When Diana came back from waving to her mom from the window, she wore that old faraway look. "You have that look that says you weren't ready to say good-bye to mommy." She smiled a half smile. "Sometimes mommies have to say good-bye too soon and you have to say good-bye too fast." Diana grasped my hand. It must have felt good to be understood.

Later in the day, Diana was constructing a body of clay. "I made a girl . . . arms, legs, eyes, nose, and a tushie." She said it with awe. I had the feeling that now Diana had a greater sense of herself as a separate person. She has all these separate parts. This was an important observation of her.

12/18 Both my assistant and I feel that she is more ready to be in the group now. She has begun to move away from adults and play with children.

12/22 Diana is really blooming these days. She seems to experience herself as a separate person. I feel that since I started this log she has been gaining strength. The log has helped me focus on Diana and give her more of the support she needs.

Through this log we see Diana emerging from her silence and her "good" exterior, becoming a person related to others and more comfortable with herself. Her growth occurred because her teacher fully believed that separation was a significant part of the curriculum for this child. The teacher's use of her own interactions with Diana, her empathy with how Diana was feeling, her one-to-one reading of books, her use of puppets, and her attention to the ritual of good-bye were all concrete actions that formed curriculum. This log illustrates that curriculum for young children is what is planned, what is thought, and what happens.

Have you any such "good" children in your group? Did you ever think that part of them, in a sense, never came to school—that part of them stayed home? Can you devise ways through your relationship with such children to test out this theory?

Perhaps your own diary of observed events in the school life of such a child would help you focus on the child's progress and on your role.

DELAYED REACTION: CHILDREN WHO ARE "FINE," THEN FALL APART

How does the curriculum serve children who seem "fine" the first few days or weeks and then fall apart? What can you do? Some of the same things that strengthened 3-year-old Diana are appropriate:

- Reading one-on-one
- Holding their hands during transition times when they may be feeling lost
- Holding them on your lap when they seem low
- Sitting close to them at eating times
- Talking with them often
- Singing with them
- Playing with them frequently

The soothing and sensitive response of an infant or toddler's primary caregiver to both baby and parent is an important curriculum support in situations like this.

You may fear that attention to one child will jeopardize your relationship with the other children. On the contrary, the others will feel reassured when they see you ministering to one child's needs. It is when a distressed child is not appropriately attended that other children become anxious and worried. We can expect children to have jealous feelings, but they will also feel that you can take care of them, too, if they are feeling unhappy.

Suppose you do all these things and none work. A child is still upset, crying, without joy or pleasure in your classroom. This may signal that perhaps he or she needs the added boost of a parent's presence in the classroom again. If the parents are free to come back (or have a flexible work schedule), they may be of two minds. One is that they are willing to help their child in any way that seems reasonable, as Kelly's mother was able to do (see Chapter 3). The other may be that the child must "get over it" and that if the parent comes back, it will only make the problem worse. A teacher may believe that, too.

In the case where a parent's return makes the situation worse, it may be that the child is not ready for a group experience at all. In such a case it might be better to suggest delaying the entry for a short time. As pointed out in Chapter 3, what is truly difficult in such a situation is helping the parent and the child, and possibly yourself, to recognize that none of you has "failed." Adults often have definite ideas that equate "growing up" with "school." It is very hard to accept the inability to go to preschool or kindergarten in any terms other than failure. However, there is no such thing as failure in early education entry. There may be only a slipping back, which requires help.

If a parent is working or is unable to return to the classroom, more creative measures will be required. The teacher will be dramatically thrust into the role of a surrogate parent and may even find that the child's difficulties are a source of great emotional drain.

Here are some actions that may help the child whose parents are unable to be with him or her:

- Arranging phone calls from the parent to the child during the day
- Keeping available a favorite object from home, something belonging to the parent such as a scarf or a purse, or a small book of photographs of the family
- Visiting the child's home in the evening
- Holding additional parent-teacher conversations and conferences
- Finding out what the child's favorite home activities are and doing them in school.
- Providing the child with a recording of the parent reading a favorite story or singing a familiar song.

Sometimes a teacher's support could be very important to a parent in talking to his or her employer about the need for a bit of time off to help her child.

IS IT REGRESSION OR TEMPERAMENT?

As pointed out in Chapter 3, it is common, in the beginning weeks or months of early care and education, to see children thumb-sucking, having toilet accidents, talking very little or too much, not eating at all or overeating, becoming clumsy, clinging to a special object, refusing to nap, crying, becoming aggressive, showing a lack of self-confidence, or being unable or unwilling to play.

We can look at these behaviors not only as regressions but also through the lens of temperament. Temperament, defined as "biologically rooted individual differences in behavior tendencies that are present early in life" (Bates, cited in Wachs, 2004, p. 12) has been described as the *how* of behavior (Chess & Thomas, 1987). Although three patterns of temperament attributes—the easy child, the difficult child, and the slow-to-warm-up child—have been identified by Chess and Thomas and are familiar to many early childhood teachers, recent work alerts us to the interaction of temperament with culture and parental beliefs. How parents regard their child's shy temperament, for example, is influenced by their socialization goals.

> In China, teachers viewed shy, sensitive children as socially and academically competent. In North America, teachers viewed shy, sensitive children as lonely and depressed. In Sweden, shy, socially reserved behavior was not consistently associated with any negative long-term outcomes, yet in North America, such behavior was found to hinder careers. (Carlson, Feng, & Harwood, 2004, p. 22)

These same authors urge that we use "less judgmental" language to describe temperament, suggesting descriptors such as " 'careful,' 'cautious,' and 'reserved' . . . that avoid negative connotations while allowing clear understanding of temperament characteristics" (p. 28).

Perhaps the child who refuses to eat or nap hits other children or doesn't engage in play has a temperament requiring focused care. Some children are more sensitive to separation than others. Some children are more outgoing than others. Some are shy. We must keep in mind that "Temperament is not immutable but may change over time. In one longitudinal study about 25% of extremely shy toddlers were found to be more outgoing at the age of 7" (Kagan, Reznick, & Snidman, cited in Carlson, Feng, & Harwood, 2004, p. 28).

While some children express their feelings openly, others are restrained. Some infants were found to be *more* withdrawn 6 months after entry. "Inhibited, self-soothing infants may be especially vulnerable because they are easy to ignore, even in relatively high-quality settings" (Fein, 1995, p. 274).

In a description of a difficult adjustment of a 3-month-old infant in a high school care center, we learn that it took 6 months of work between the teen mother, the primary caregiver, and the director to resolve the problem (Elliot, 2003). Initially, in September the caregiver used a series of strategies with the agitated infant, including wrapping the baby tightly (swaddling), covering her head with a blanket to reduce stimulation, using a "white noise" machine, rocking, crooning, and taking the baby outdoors, hoping fresh air would calm her. Because these techniques helped for only a short time, the mother was often summoned from her class to calm the baby. Finally, in January, a new plan for the mother produced a more regular, predictable arrival and departure, during which times the primary caregiver played with the baby while sitting close to the mother. This was reassuring to the baby. Nevertheless, it took until March for the baby to feel totally safe in another's care. Although we would expect a smoother transition for such a young baby, Kagan and Snidman (cited in Elliot, 2003) found that approximately 10% of infants "show high levels of motor activity and crying in response to novelty at four months of age and do not welcome change, new people, or strange situations" (p. 27).

Truly, *all* young children need some measure of adult help during the separation process to avoid feeling abandoned. Whether due to regression or temperament, the behavioral challenge to teachers remains the same. No matter what kinds of signals a child sends out, your support and understanding are critical. A child, who is behaving in an unloveable manner, is the one who needs the most loving attention. Since temperament is very central to a child's adaptation to other-than-mother care, adjustment in the behavior and attitudes of teachers and caregivers is necessary.

CHILDREN WITH SPECIAL NEEDS

Children have a variety of needs stemming from particular circumstances. For example, some children come from single-parent homes, from homes with recently separated parents, from homes where there has been a death or chronic or serious illness of a loved person or pet. Some children's parents may be depressed, retarded, mentally ill, or adolescent. Some children have mental, emotional, or physical disabilities. Any such circumstance may influence the quality of the parent-child separation. Teachers need to be especially sensitive to these children and parents. While it is true that their differences should be minimized rather than exaggerated, children and parents may require special attention as they separate.

In a program for children who are mildly retarded, for example, it was noted that the children did not give the same kinds of clues to their feelings about separation as did nonretarded children (Kessler, Ablon, & Smith, 1969). Their regressive behavior was often attributed to the retardation itself, and the children's aimless running around to hyperactivity. As the teachers helped the mothers recognize their children's feelings of anxiety about separation, the mothers began to understand the depth of their children's attachment. The teachers also made special efforts to identify a child to himself by "showing him his own photograph, saying his name and verbally calling attention to what he was doing" (p. 6). Then they attempted to develop in the child the same awareness of "mother." They talked about "where she is now, what she is doing, and the reunion with her" (p. 7). The teachers continually encouraged the expected, normal response to separation on the part of the children, and in so doing enlisted the mothers' cooperation. Concretizing the separation process and a child's identity helped these children, since they lacked conceptualizing skills.

Notwithstanding their disabilities, children are predisposed to become attached to their parents and to experience separation reactions (Cicchetti & Beeghly, 1990; Erickson & Kurz-Riemer, 1999), although there may be a delay in its expression (Foley, 1986). Their cues are often subtle and difficult to read. On the other hand, a child may display obvious separation anxiety if she or he had previously been admitted to the hospital many times and subjected to painful procedures (Zelle & Coyner, 1983). As children's emotional growth takes place, however, they may begin to understand the meaning of their parent's putting on a coat or jacket.

The transition from an early intervention program to preschool, or from home-based to center-based care affects the whole family. Changes occur in schedules, in transportation, and in the close relationships formed with teachers, therapists, nurses, and social workers (Hains, Rosenkoetter, & Fowler, 1991). Parents, the sole protectors of their children who have endured countless medical issues, have concerns about the child's safety in the new program:

- Is this a safe place?
- Is the bus safe?
- Will the child fall down?
- Will she get hurt?

- Will people understand him? He has a language delay.
- How will the staff manage her eating and toileting?

And in the case of some children, it's devastating to parents when the child is unable to wave goodbye.

Months of advance planning are often required because the changes in roles and expectations are a source of stress (McDonald, Kyselka, & Siebert, 1989). Some stress is alleviated by visits to the new program before the child's entry (Rosenkoetter & Rosenkoetter, 1993). During the visit staff is able to answer parents' questions before the child starts the program. In addition, a support network with other parents whose children have disabilities is initiated.

I asked the staff of an inclusionary[1] program for infants and toddlers about some factors that aid separation. They had helpful ideas. For example, they found that some children with disabilities profited from a very structured goodbye.

> Darrin (age 2) followed the same routine with his mother each morning: one kiss, one hug, one squeeze, in that order, first in the room and then again at the door.

A book of photographs of the day's routines served as a visual reminder of the program's predictability. In support of parents, the staff set up a specific day and time each week when parents could call the primary caregiver. In addition, the staff created a "Communication Book" that went back and forth each day between home and center. It contained observations and comments written by teachers, therapists, and parents. Teachers wrote:

> Shanice was very sad this morning when her dad left but when her friend Maria came in she brightened.
> Frankie was able to accept comfort from me after he got off the bus. Then he played with play dough and made a birthday cake.

Parents wrote:

> His turtleneck shirt is missing.
> Last night she didn't sleep well. Make sure she gets enough lunch.
> He's been lining up his toys in long rows. What does that mean?

---

1. The term *inclusionary* describes a program that includes children with disabilities along with those developing typically.

Children with special needs and their families require special thought and attention when the issue is separation.

ADULT BEHAVIORS THAT HELP CHILDREN COPE WITH SEPARATION

There are many ways to help children express their feelings about separation and cope with their emotions. The *key* to working with young children and babies as they enter early care and education is to communicate that it *is ok* to feel sad, frightened, or angry. In legitimizing these feelings, you build self-confidence and trust. This is just the opposite of conventional wisdom that dictates "don't talk about it."

> Grandfather hugs 26-month-old Eli, says goodbye, and leaves. Eli grabs a paper towel from the nearby dispenser and yanks hard. He vigorously throws the towel on the floor and stamps his foot. Nora, his primary caregiver, softly says, "Oh, Eli, you are so angry that grandfather left." Nora stays close to him as he continues pulling and throwing towels on the floor. After a few minutes he walks away from the pile of towels, looks up at Nora, and says, "I go paint."

If young children are worried about where their parents are, or worried about feeling angry, they will not be able to use their energy for the normal pursuits of learning and exploration. In trying to distract children or otherwise minimize their anxious feelings, you send a message that their emotions are not authentic. However, when you validate these emotions, as Nora did, you contribute to a child's sense of power. In successfully contending with a difficult situation, children learn that adults are reliable.

Encouraging expressions of emotion, through both words and actions, is an investment in children's growth. In the words of one expert, "The child who really copes well allows himself to miss the absent loved one, to feel sad, lonely and perhaps angry, and to express his feelings appropriately" (Furman, 1974, p. 16).

What are some special strategies that are useful for giving children comfort during these first few weeks and help them move toward self-confidence?

- Encourage children to participate fully in saying goodbye. Hugging, kissing, crying, waving, and saying, "I'll miss you" are all ways of bringing feelings out into the open. Once in the open, they are easier to deal with. *A parent should never sneak out.*

- Plan together—parents, teachers, and children—for the next day's parting. Will the child walk with the parent to the door? Make a drawing for the parent to take along? Will the parent read one story? Through such planning children gain security and experience self-confidence.
- Provide an opportunity for children to watch parents leave. Teachers and parents can choose a window in the classroom through which children can peer. Steps placed by a high window allow children to look into the street as parents leave the building, look up, and wave goodbye.
- Regard all the "baby ways" that may appear, from thumb-sucking to wet pants, without a fuss. The less attention you pay to such behaviors, even if you do not like them, the sooner they will disappear.
- Be aware of transition times in the daily classroom schedule, such as cleanup periods or moving from one activity to another. Sometimes those "in-between times" are especially difficult for children who are coping with separation. They may go out of control, hit other children, withdraw, suck their thumbs, or masturbate. Try to involve a child in activity right away.
- Recognize that Mondays and Fridays are often hard days because they involve parting *from parents* (*Monday*) and *from the center/school* (*Friday*). And don't forget the day after (or before) a holiday break.
- Encourage children to bring a favorite toy or blanket to school each day, or something belonging to their parents. Allow them *not* to share these "security" objects. To the children, they are a bit of home.

A reminder to caregivers of infants and toddlers—when leaving the room to go to the bathroom, getting more supplies from the closet in the hall, or taking a regular break, be sure to announce, "I'll be right back." Children under three often equate an adult leaving the room with the departure of their own parent.

ACTIVITIES THAT SUPPORT CHILDREN

Specific activities can engage young children's coping abilities and help them realize that while home and program are separate, home is not forgotten.

Creating Wall Displays

A list of children's names and birthdays on a kindergarten or preschool wall chart will attract the attention of children and their parents. What a sure message to children that the teacher really wants them! If the names are printed large, with a felt-tip marker, children who are able to recognize their own names will feel pleased. Children who do not read will feel equally delighted when their parents point out their names.

A wall poster in an infant/toddler room announcing the names of each child's family members, including pets, welcomes parents and children. It helps parents to know one another's names. Such a welcome eases the entry to the center by making a firm connection to home.

Writing Letters

Writing a letter to the parent from the child is meaningful to 3-, 4-, and 5-year-olds. Setting down "Come back soon," "I miss you," or "I love you" in words on paper seems to be very reassuring. The letter can contain a drawing or the child's own "writing" and can be tucked away in the child's cubby to be shared, or not, when the parent comes back. It will be up to the child to decide.

Displaying Photographs

Photographs of children's families, including pets, posted in an accessible spot help young children remember that their families really do exist, even though they cannot be seen. If these photographs are covered with clear adhering plastic, they will withstand lots of loving attention. Be sure they are hung at children's eye level so that they can be seen easily. If they are attached to a board with velcro, the children can take them off and carry them around as needed.

> A teacher of toddlers gathers the children together each morning for a short circle time. She holds up a photo of one child at a time, asking, "Who is this?" Some children call out the name, especially the picture child who then takes the photo and presses it to the velcro on a large board. They sing, "Good morning to Jody, good morning to you. . . ." And go on to the next photo.

A special book of photographs about life at home may help ease the transition from home to program and provide an opportunity for parents to be involved. A child could take the book home each afternoon and bring it back in the morning.

A picture of the family tucked into a child's lunch box brings a warm reminder of home.

Cooking

Cooking activities link young children to home in a very concrete fashion. Nothing could be more familiar than food and its preparation, except its consumption. Cooking with children is a natural way to bring home and school together while at the same time creating opportunities for competent action and intellectual investigations. Shaping the cookies, mixing the batter, cutting vegetables for soup, dipping bread into an egg-milk mixture for French toast, and peeling then slicing a banana with a tongue depressor are all activities that allow even the youngest children to share the enticing world of adults. Here also are chances for mind stretching—reading recipes, calculating quantities, measuring, predicting outcomes (e.g., What will happen to the flour when we add the milk?), and engaging the senses. Powerful connections with home are forged when a family member actually comes into the classroom to help a cooking group or to teach them how to create a special dish.

How do cooking activities help children resolve their separation conflicts?

Playing

As described in great detail in Chapter 3, both teachers and parents need to provide for, and observe, the natural make-believe play of 1- to 5-year-old children. This will give consistent clues as to how children are doing in their attempts to cope with separation reactions. Children may play baby or nurturing parent many times over in their attempts to come to terms with their feelings. They may play themes of moving or going away on a train, car, or a plane. They may play monster as they begin to face their fears of being on their own in school or center. Provide for this play by supplying props such as cast-off telephones, suitcases, steering wheels, dolls, a doll bed large enough for a child to lie in, and, most important, time, space, and privacy for play. By listening to and observing such play, you

Taking on a role enables children to experiment with another identity while strengthening their own.

will discover the means children use to cope with their feelings and their thoughts.

A teacher can read a story to some preschool-age children, such as *Amos and Boris* (Steig, 1971), which is about the parting of two dear animal friends. Then an environment can be created for them to act it out on their own terms as described by Vivian Paley (2004). The children will assign roles to one another and decide among themselves how the story will be played. It will be *their interpretation*, not a re-creation of what was just read.

Another form of make-believe that is meaningful to preschoolers of ages 3, 4, and 5 is puppet play. Using puppets may help children express their feelings of longing for their parents. Children this age are attracted by soft animal puppets and can project themselves into the puppet. Often they label the puppet "mommy," "daddy," "grandma," or "baby." Adults can help children by using a puppet to ask their puppets questions, such as, Do you go to school? What do you play with when you are at school? When you are at the center, what is your mommy (daddy, grandma) doing? Do you have a baby in your house? Who takes care of your baby? Adults may be included in the play and perhaps assigned a role. (Remember that although toddlers are very attracted to puppets, it is beyond their developmental capacity to project themselves into the puppet for this form of play.)

Even so humble a game as ball play can serve to soothe a child's separation emotion. Not only a preschooler or toddler, but also a baby who is now able to sit steadily, can get emotional profit from rolling a ball back and forth with an adult. This social play clearly represents the "goodbye" and "hello" of parental departure. Using those very words as you play this game will make that association available to the child.

And don't forget the old-fashioned jack-in-the-box toy to act out "you're gone, you're back!" with all the excitement of waiting for the music to end and the jack to jump up!

In a large cardboard appliance box, cut out a door and windows for peekaboo play. Make a "peekaboo board" with family photos. Cover each picture with a piece of cloth that can be lifted up to say "Hi, mommy." (For these and other peek-a-boo ideas, see Szamreta, 2003.)

Games of peek-a-boo, covering your face (or the toddler's face) with a cloth, and games of hiding and retrieval can be played in sand and water where small toys can be hidden and found easily. Hide-and-seek, chase, "gonna get'cha" are more active forms of the same game. These are all ways of practicing, recapitulating, and getting a grip on being left and being reunited. Such games give children control over the process of leaving and returning. Don't underestimate the power of peek-a-boo for young children. It's not only a game for babies.

Twenty-one-month-old Ishmail hugged teacher Wendy, raced across the room and ducked behind the sheer curtain of the adult coat closet. "Where's Ishmail?" sang out Wendy. Thrusting the curtain aside, a grinning Ishmail pops out and runs back to Wendy's arms. They play this enchanting game at least 10 times.

Providing Expressive Materials

Provide nonstructured materials such as paints, blocks, clay, crayons, felt-tip markers, and clean drawing paper. This allows children to spontaneously represent their feelings about themselves, their families, and their entry into the new world of school. Some of those feelings may not be pleasant, and it will help if you are prepared to see both angry and sad feelings being displayed.

Reading Books

Storybooks about how it feels to be separated from a loved one can open the way for children and adults to talk together about separation and to gain new insights into the process.

Choosing these books should be done with care. The first consideration is that the book be good literature. It should be pleasurable to read and pleasurable to hear. Does the book display clarity of writing style, brevity, interesting characters, and suitable illustrations? Is the story related to the child's own life experiences? Do children see people like themselves? Is the book in their language? Be certain that the book is free from stereotypes. It must also appeal to adults—it is very unsatisfying to read to children if the book is uninteresting to the reader.

Books that address sensitive topics like separation need other special qualities. In an article about the use of books in crisis situations, adults are urged to apply the following guidelines:

> Can children identify with the plot, setting, dialogue, and characters? . . .
> Does the book use correct terminology, psychologically sound explanations, and portray events accurately? . . .
> Are the origins of emotional reactions revealed and inspected? . . .
> Does the book reflect an appreciation for individual differences? . . .
> Does the book present crises in an optimistic, surmountable fashion? (Jalongo, 1983, p. 32)

How you read a book to children is critical. First, be thoroughly familiar with the book before you read it to a child. Next, introduce it briefly by

Children make an impact on a blank piece of paper. It is a way of saying, "I am me—a separate, special person."

Using expressive materials encourages concentration and sensory experience.

Satisfaction, a feeling of accomplishment, and a sense of competence come from the joyful involvement with nonstructured materials. How does this activity help children cope with separation?

referring to a naturally occurring situation that may have prompted its use. Asking specific questions throughout, or after, the story "encourages children to analyze the behavior of the story characters, make inferences about emotional reactions, apply information to their own experience, and synthesize techniques for coping with crisis" (p. 34). Finally, summarize the story by rephrasing the basic story concepts. In this way, children's ideas and information can be clarified.

An annotated list of books for children about separation and entry into early care and education can be found in Appendix A at the end of the book.

Other Ways to Help

There are other ways you can help children achieve control of the separation process. Here are some suggestions:

- If a program has a before-school opening "paint and get ready" spruce-up session in which parents contribute some working assistance, include children in some appropriate work. They can put the clean toys on the shelves, wash tables and chairs, help mount pictures, or label cubbies. This activity adds a measure of child control over the physical environment and affords them some familiarity

Reading to a child alone, or in a small, intimate group, gives children a close experience of being nurtured at a time when they may be feeling in need of special care.

with the room. Teachers, children, and parents can begin to know one another.

- During beginning days, children can choose the spot in the room for their parents to sit.
- A child can be asked to decide when his or her parent should leave the room. Shall it be now, or after snack?
- When the group goes outdoors, a child can be asked to say goodbye to a parent who then stays in the room. This reverses the process, allowing the child, rather than the parent, to do the leaving.
- Once a child is secure in the classroom, a teacher can encourage her capacity to separate through a variety of small separation experiences. For example, the teacher can ask the child to return a few lunch dishes to the kitchen, take a message to another teacher, or visit another classroom for a short period of time to hear a story or paint a picture.
- Whenever a child first enters an ongoing group, be sure to announce to all the children how happy you are to welcome the newcomer.

In one ongoing early care program for infants and toddlers, the teacher sings a hello song when the new parent-baby pair come into the room for the first few times. Since this program practices a slow, gradual entry, the baby leaves earlier than the other children for the first 2 weeks. When the pair leaves the room to go home, the teachers and children sing a goodbye song that ends with "See you tomorrow." Hellos and goodbyes are bottom-line important.

BEGINNING DAYS IN A PROGRAM

Beginning days and weeks are not the time for exciting trips or stimulating art projects. Children need time to get acquainted with the teachers and with the room and its materials. Careful planning for these beginning days is a necessity. As a teacher, you have many decisions to make.

- Do you want to put out all the blocks or just a limited number of shapes? Think about the age of the children and their former experience with blocks. Very young children of 3 and younger may be overwhelmed by more than just three or four basic shapes in the beginning. On the other hand, kindergarteners, who may be experienced builders, might feel cheated if the block shelves were not full.
- Will you start with several colors of paint or just one or two? Do you want to start with paint at all? Young toddlers may not be ready to use brushes and an easel in the early days of the program. They may need more time to control their small muscles, while older children may be ready right away to try their hands at painting.
- Do you want to have hard as well as easy puzzles on the shelf? Are some of the children entering your group highly skilled in puzzles? You will need to think about children who may get discouraged if they try puzzles that are out of their range.
- Will you provide paste with collage materials or will you wait until the children have been in the program for a while? Your decision may be based on the age and experience of the children as well as the amount of adult help you have in the room. If you have to spend a lot of time teaching children how to use paste, it may inhibit you from interacting with parents and children as freely as you wish.
- Will you put out crayons or felt-tip markers with paper, or both? Markers are very easy to use and respond best to a light touch. Think about the age of your children and the kind of touch they use. The younger the child, the heavier the touch. An 18-month-old does not have the finesse of a 5-year-old.

These decisions will convey specific messages to children and their parents. A carefully arranged room with well-chosen materials in appropriate quantities reflects your serious attention to the needs of beginning days. When there is a certain order, a cheerful cleanliness, an array of attractive playthings that are not overwhelming, this will tell those entering your room that you have anticipated their arrival joyfully—and thoughtfully. Your pleasure, and your care, in their entry will prepare the way for a successful separation.

SOCIAL LIFE

The social life of an early childhood classroom is a slowly evolving, ever-changing phenomenon. Today's enemies are tomorrow's friends. "You can't come to my birthday" frequently turns into "Do you want to play good guys and bad guys?" Teachers play an important role in helping young children learn what it means to be a friend when they demonstrate friendliness, compassion, and respect for children. This model of an adult who is an enabler (Katz, 1977) provides the most meaningful lesson to the young. In an atmosphere of acceptance, children learn to be accepting; in an atmosphere of empathy, children learn to be empathic; in an atmosphere that encourages autonomy, children learn to be autonomous.

The understanding of social life develops as children's thinking abilities mature. In a study of friendship, children's ideas were shown to change as they became less egocentric[2] (Selman & Selman, 1979). Whereas in early childhood a friend may be regarded as valuable because "she has a new action figure toy," children develop, by early teens, an understanding of the reciprocal nature of friendship.

Helping children as they struggle to comprehend what it means to get along with others is a demanding task. It is often more helpful for the children to be asked, "What's happening?" in a conflict situation than for the adult to decide who is at fault. Children need the opportunity to examine a situation and try to work out a solution with the adult's help. They need as much chance to play alone as with others because social life requires that people be in harmony with themselves as a foundation to harmony with others.

Although babies under 1 year old demonstrate keen interest in other babies, wiggling their arms and bodies with excitement when a small "friend"

---

2. *Egocentric* is a term that describes young children's thinking. It is characterized by the assumption that the actions of people and events in the child's world are somehow magically connected to the child's self (ego). For example, a 3-year-old eager to see snow asked, "If I take a nap, will it snow?" as though her napping could influence a natural event.

Making friends becomes possible when a trust of adults exists at a deep level. Only then is it safe to reach out to others and to commit oneself to the classroom world. Sometimes friendship takes unique forms.

arrives for the day, true friendships appear sometime after the first birthday when a toddler is able to recognize a peer as a social partner (Howes, 2000). These stable, reciprocal toddler relationships help youngsters develop social interaction skills and provide them with emotional support, helping to alleviate some distress of the day-long separation from parents (Lieberman, 1993). Studies show that when children transition to a new classroom, they fare better when they move with friends (Howes, 2000). Friendships "may serve as a 'secure base' from which to explore and cope with novel surroundings and demands" (Ladd, 1990, p. 1082). These friendships serve as "peer attachments" (Howes, 1988, p. 66), fostering feelings of safety and security that help children cope with the demands of new early care and education environments.

In some infant/toddler settings, children age 18 to 24 months make the transition from an infant to a toddler group, a separation that requires careful planning. At one center, Daniel (1993) describes a toddler's very gradual move to the new room over a 5- to 6-week period, accompanied by the primary caregiver. She compares the transition to climbing a mountain in which the learner needs the attention and support of the expert as he climbs, slips, falters, and is scared (Foley, cited in Daniel, 1993). Although the staff stays in constant touch with the parent, it is not until the move is complete that the parent then takes the child to the new room. This helps to maintain the infant room as the secure base during the transition.

Preschool is a setting for the emergence, development, and maintenance of a peer culture that speaks to 3-, 4-, and 5-year-olds' gaining control over their own lives (Corsaro & Eder, 1990). Resistance to and challenging adult authority is a central theme in the peer culture that pertains directly to the issue of separation from parents. Children in a peer culture construct meaning together in their "attempts *to deal with confusions, concerns, fears, and conflicts* in their daily lives" (1990, p. 214). Corsaro (2003) describes the experiences of preschool children engaged in "approach-avoidance" games in which there is a monster, witch, or other menacing figure.

> In approach-avoidance play and games we saw a routine that might be a universal feature of kids' cultures. Here, the threatened kids are always in charge and they collectively produce a routine in which they share the buildup of tension, the excitement of the threat, and the relief and joy of the escape. Furthermore, in approach-avoidance play, kids' social representations of danger, evil, and the unknown are more firmly grasped and controlled. And all of this occurs while kids are playing and having fun, creating their own peer cultures, and preparing themselves for fuller participation in the adult world. (p. 65)

Adults help young children define their separating selves by encouraging them to interact constructively with other children and by taking these interactions seriously. By respecting and sustaining the peer culture, you build a bridge connecting children securely to the human world.

ENCOURAGING CHILDREN'S COMPETENCE

Through a curriculum that has an understructure of support for separating children, teachers can provide many opportunities for them to develop and exercise competence. Helping them build self-confidence and self-reliance appropriately can make them feel comfortable and safe when they are away from the protection of their parents. The key word here is *appropriately*. Even though 2-year-olds, for example, might be able to do many things for themselves, it is not appropriate to assume that they never need holding or cuddling, or that they can solve interpersonal problems without the assistance of an adult.

Competence is built in many ways in the preschool environment:

Through taking risks, developing skills, and

through engaging with books.

A child discovers himself as a builder.

The thrust to being capable, to making a difference in the world, to having an effect on the environment, comes from within. It is said that such motivation is inborn (White, 1968). You who have been with children day after day know firsthand about their intense drive to do things for themselves. "I do it myself!" is a phrase familiar to every early childhood teacher and parent. It begins when children are under 2 years of age, with their actions saying what their words cannot.

Encouraging this innate motivation builds competence in the young. There are many opportunities in the early childhood classroom for this: in carrying out the routines of the day, such as pouring juice, dressing, choosing foods to eat, or using the toilet; in selecting toys to play with or art materials to use and getting them from the shelves themselves; in taking risks, making friends, and choosing books. Achievement fills a child with pride and self-gratification. It is fed by the comfort and trust generated in a secure classroom environment. Separation is the "developmental necessity" underlying the child's discovery of himself or herself as a builder.

Whether teacher or parent, your most valuable contribution to a child's development will be the recognition that separation reactions in young children are valid and expectable. Your own knowledge and your understanding of this as a significant element of the early childhood curriculum will help children to develop a strong sense of themselves as individuals able to feel sad, angry, and grieving. They will be able to develop the ability to cope with those feelings without being overwhelmed or rendered ineffective.

The steps children take in early care and education to achieve this will help them practice the skills they will use in many different separation experiences throughout their lives (E. Furman, 1974; R. Furman, 1972).

5

Parents and Teachers: Learning Together

PARENTS, CHILDREN, AND TEACHERS are equal participants in the drama of separation and entry into early care and education. Each group has needs that require attention. This chapter addresses the needs of parents and teachers to learn from one another.

In September, newspapers often carry stories about school openings that seem to verify the meaningful nature of this event. They may include photographs that dramatize the tension of starting school for young children and their parents. The *New York Times* (Daley, 1982) reported:

> The stuffed animal that goes everywhere with 5-year-old Eric Benderisky went to Public School 9 yesterday. It was Eric's first day of school, and Puppy Dog's, too. Eric held one paw, and Eric's mother, Ruth, held the other, and that was the way they arrived at 100 West 84th Street. Eric said he was OK. His mother said she was nervous.
>
> Elizabeth Sanchez kept her eyes on her son, Jason, 6, who had complained of a stomachache before he left for school. "His older sister said some bad things to him about school, so he's scared," Mrs. Sanchez said.

Another school entry made the news (Kleiman, 1980):

> Diana Lambouras, who had taken her 5-year-old son, Emilio, to school for the first time yesterday, was standing in the rear of his classroom at P.S. 51. It was almost 2 p.m. and she had been standing there all day.
>
> "I've tried to leave," Mrs. Lambouras explained. "But every time I do, he falls on the floor and starts screaming."
>
> Mrs. Lambouras said she had asked her son this past weekend whether he wanted to go to school and when he had told her he did not, she said she had tried to change his mind.

"You'll learn to read and write, you'll make new friends," Mrs. Lambouras recalled, saying, "You want to go to school, now don't you?"

"'Yes,'" Mrs. Lambouras said her son had answered, "'but you have to come with me.'"

Mrs. Lambouras agreed.

She said she planned to stay with Emilio today and even tomorrow. . . .

"But next week," she added, "he's on his own."

PAVING THE WAY

Perhaps some form of preparation might have made this first day of kindergarten more comfortable or more predictable, such as:

- A visit to the school by the parent and child in the spring
- A meeting with the teacher prior to the school's opening
- A written description of school beginning sent to the parents
- A teacher's visit to the child's home
- A parents' meeting held before school started

Steps like these might have contributed clarity and direction to the event. Often a letter from the teacher to the child is helpful. It is very exciting for young children to receive mail. A questionnaire for parents might contribute to the home-school relationship.

With infants and toddlers it is *imperative* that contacts between teachers and parents be as ongoing, supportive, and close as those with the children. When you think "children" of this age, you also need to automatically think "parents." There can be no distinction, for the way a teacher treats the child affects the parents and the way a teacher treats the parents affects the child. Caregivers of children under age 3 must focus on both the children themselves and their attachment relationship to their parents. While a little more distance has developed between preschool children of 3, 4, and 5 and their parents, they are, nevertheless, still bound very closely together. Respect for this bond is a major part of the early care and education entry process.

Every effort should be made for teachers and parents to have contact before the children arrive in the program. Parents need to see what sort of a person the teacher is and how he or she works with children. Parents need to know some of a teacher's ideas about relating to children and decide whether or not they agree. They need to feel that a teacher is trustworthy and competent to take care of their dearest possessions.

A father stated that he was both excited and nervous when his baby started in early care. He had "a lot of questions—worry—will my toddler's individual needs be noticed? And, then, there's the long day—5 days, 9 to 5—plus the issue of his special needs. He gets Early Intervention services . . . He's high maintenance—he needs a lot of adult energy . . . he craves talking attention."

In one early care center, parents are invited to observe the teacher in action with her present class before deciding whether to enroll their child. Once they decide, the family with an infant is invited to come in before the baby's first day to select a crib and to make it up with a favorite sheet and a mobile or other toy that the baby knows well. Such a preenrollment visit is actually the beginning of the separation process and is the first phase of the entry. The message to parents is: (1) our center respects your judgment and your duty to know what kind of arrangements you are making for your child, and (2) we think our center is pretty wonderful and we want you to see it for yourself. Parents have every right to suspect that something is wrong with a program where no such visiting is allowed. This holds true for parents of 3-, 4-, and 5-year-olds as well as the under-3s.

If the parents, after an initial visit, decide they want their children in the program, teachers will have the first opportunity to get to know them. Whether a teacher arranges for a home visit or for a conference before a child's arrival depends on the preferences of the teachers and the parents.

While a home visit helps a child and family make a firm link with a program and to learn *who the teacher is*, it presents challenges. As the teacher, your purpose in visiting the home is to form a friendship with the child, but you must, at the same time, connect with the parent. If you feel anxious or uncomfortable about the visit, consider asking a coworker to accompany you.

As a parent, you may find the idea of a home visit nerve-wracking. You may feel that you will be judged on the basis of how your living quarters look. Or you may consider it an invasion of your privacy. Some families thoroughly enjoy the sociability of the occasion.

When you, as a teacher, make a home visit, you are a guest in a stranger's house. Can you remain without judgment when you see how others live differently from yourself? One child may live in an extended family with two or three generations in one space. Another may live with gay or lesbian parents, a foster family, or a single mother or father. One family may require you to "break bread" with them as a sign of respect. Where one family may have the most meager of furnishings, another may have the most sumptuous. Some families are neat, everything in its place. Others are haphazard, with stacks of papers or objects strewn throughout. Some families have dogs or other pets. What if you don't speak their language, and they don't speak yours? What if several neighbors are invited in to meet you when you arrive?

If you feel that a parent is not comfortable with a home visit, consider an alternative such as meeting the child and parent at a playground, park, or local ice-cream shop (teacher's treat). (For further suggestions about home visiting, see Johnston & Mermin, 1994.)

This first face-to-face contact is the second step in the entry and separation process. What might take place? Think about what a teacher would want to find out about the children and their families. What might parents wish to learn from the teacher? Should parents be asked to fill out a questionnaire to supplement the conference?

> Ms. Kraft arrived for her first meeting with the teacher. Her 3-year-old son Aaron would be starting at the center the following week. The teacher outlined the first week's schedule, explaining that he welcomed and hoped that Ms. Kraft could stay in the classroom with Aaron at least the first day. He invited Ms. Kraft to the first parents' meeting for which she had already received an invitation.
>
> "How are you feeling about Aaron's beginning school?" the teacher asked.
>
> "Well, to tell you the truth," Ms. Kraft answered, "I'm excited. It's wonderful to see him becoming so independent and so grown up. But I'm a little nervous, too. You know it's a new phase in our lives. I'm so used to leaving him at home with the babysitter when I'm at work. And I don't think my boss will let me take the day off to stay in the classroom."
>
> "Other mothers have told me the same thing. So you can see that you're not alone in your feelings. Do you think your babysitter, or someone who knows your son well, could stay with him for a time in the beginning?"
>
> "Well, I'm sure he'll be fine without me, but I suppose that the sitter, or my mother, could spend some time with him to help him get used to it here."

The teacher and Ms. Kraft have just started to build their relationship. The teacher raised the issue of separation so that Ms. Kraft would have the opportunity to prepare herself and her son. He tried to make Ms. Kraft feel that her slight nervousness and her inability to stay were not unusual. Ms. Kraft was trying to make the teacher feel that her son would be a "good boy." The groundwork had been set for the teacher and parent to begin to work together.

Had it been possible for this parent to stay with her child—if she worked evenings or part time or was a stay-at-home mom—the teacher would have worked out a transition to the classroom that would fit her schedule.

On the other hand, if it were *not* possible for anyone else to stay with the child, the teacher would need to forge a plan. First, he or she would need to ascertain the child's possible reaction to the parent's leaving. If it were feasible, he might consider assigning a primary caregiver to bridge the gap. He would request that the child bring a favorite toy from home, and would arrange a special phone call from the parent to the child during the day. It would be important for him to be especially alert to this child. It would *not* be wise, however, to allow the parent of an infant or toddler to leave a young baby without a phase-in period. Small babies and their parents are too vulnerable for such a "drop-and-run" approach.

What if a parent has never left the child with anyone but family and insists that a cousin, grandparent, or aunt stays with the child, feeds lunch, and puts the child down for a nap? In families where interdependence is dominant over independence, leaving a child with a stranger may be uncomfortable. It is the teacher's role to help such a family move slowly into the new culture of the early care and education program without a rupture of respect.

The essence of all arrangements for the phase-in period is flexibility. A rigid method tends to create conflicts and misunderstanding.

CHILDREN ARE STRANGERS

When children come to early care and education for the first time, they are strangers. As a teacher, you know very little about them. They know very little about you. You have not had time yet to become sensitive to their cues. You have not become alert yet to that "look in Tina's eyes" telling you that a storm may break.

During these beginning days you may have very little information to guide you, for children have many different ways of telling you how they feel. Each one has his or her own behavior vocabulary. For example, two children may feel angry. One child may scream in rage; another may withdraw into a quiet, sullen shell. As you come to know the children by means of your observations and your contact throughout the year, you begin to know which behavior, for which child, means what most of the time.

Perhaps you depend on your intuition and former experiences to cope with the range of feelings that you see a child express. Sometimes you will probably be right in what you surmise and what you decide to do. Sometimes you will probably be wrong. Much of what you do in the beginning will be guesswork. For that reason, it is crucial at a child's entry to enlist support of the parents, who truly know the child best.

PARENTS AS A SOURCE OF INFORMATION

The first meeting with parents held either before or as children begin in a program is vital for a teacher to learn about the children. It will establish the tone of the program's relationship with the family and will influence the nature of exchanges throughout the year. Parents and teachers will each begin to form an opinion of one another. It is up to both of you to set this tone by your friendliness, your openness, and your ability to listen and to withhold judgment.

In this first exchange, a teacher will be able to learn about the parents' concerns and wishes for their child. The parents will be able to sense a teacher's interest in them as well as in their son or daughter.

A teacher can gain important information about children from this first meeting by posing thoughtful questions for parents, such as:

- What brought you to seek a program for your child at this time?
- What are your wishes and aspirations for Taka?

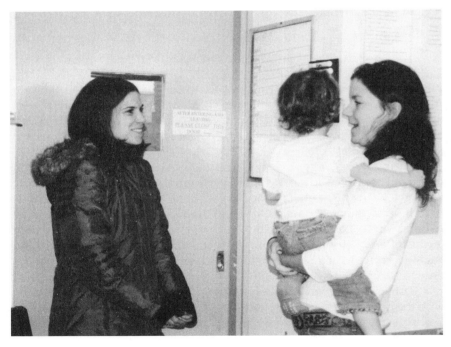

Informally exchanged information at pickup and drop-off times encourages the teacher's and parent's relationship.

- What would you like me to know about Ashlee's development?
- What can you tell me about Tyrone's pattern of eating and sleeping? About his usual routine at home?
- How would you describe Esperanza's personality and disposition? What do you like most about her? Is there anything about her that you would like to change?

A teacher's task in this first interview will be twofold; first, to learn what the parents think about their children by listening carefully to how they talk about them, and second, to help parents think about their decision to send their child to your program. You can do this by describing your program so parents can decide whether or not they have made the right choice.

You may get the impression that some parents are not comfortable discussing matters about their children that they consider private. They may perceive these questions as "prying." In that case, hold off, assure the parent that you are happy to have her child in your group and that you look forward to getting to know them both as time goes on.

PROVIDING HELP FOR PARENTS AND CHILDREN WHEN THE PROGRAM BEGINS

Parents are reassured when a teacher welcomes them to stay with their children for the beginning day or days, or as long as they believe it necessary. While some parents may worry that they will not be allowed to stay at all, others may worry that they will be required to stay too long or that their children will never stay unless they leave the building immediately.

Here are some ways in which teachers help parents strike a balance— neither too short nor too long a stay.

- Discuss the entry process and raise the issue of separation in your initial interview, either when the parent seeks information about the program or before the program starts. If feasible, reinforce this with a phone call before the child arrives for the first day. Perhaps the parent has last-minute questions or concerns. This contact is especially important for parents of infants because putting an infant in out-of-home care is very gut-wrenching.
- Be a good listener. What are parents really saying? Are they nervous about separation? Are they receptive to your ideas? Do they minimize the impact of separation? Are they reluctant to participate in a separation process because they must go to work or because

they reject the concept itself? Do they need more information? Are they concerned that their children will never separate if they stay in the room? Do they suggest "slipping out" while the children are occupied? You must decide how you will handle these questions (some of them are discussed later in the chapter).

- Reassure parents that you will work as partners with them for the benefit of their children. You can let them know that you will take your cues from them since they know their children best. Some parents may need to hear that you will not require them to stay any longer than necessary, especially if a child has been in a program before— or if he or she is the second, third, or fourth child in the family.
- Have a plan for the first week, or weeks, based on the age and needs of the children and the needs of the parents. The younger the children, the more time will probably be needed for them to feel safe. A plan that is worked out with the entire staff of the school or center offers consistency to parents. Chapter 6, on school policy, contains some guidelines for forming such plans.
- Support parents when it is impossible for them to attend with their children and have a plan to communicate with them each day of the entry period. Sometimes an additional daily phone call or two from the parent at work to the child at the center helps ameliorate loneliness.

When you provide supportive help to parents, in most cases they will respond with information about themselves and their children that will contribute to your effectiveness. You will learn from them, through the support and help you give them.

PARENTS IN THE CLASSROOM

Further support for a teacher's efforts to learn about the children from their parents will come through the parents' presence in the classroom during the first days of the children's attendance. Parents have intimate information about their children, such as the following:

He'll stay by my side for a while watching what the other children do, but then he'll make his way over to something that interests him.
She's such a social butterfly! You'll see that in no time at all she'll be talking up a storm with another child.
We're really going to have trouble with Randy. He never wants me to leave him. I don't know what I'm going to do.

Other parents may be more circumspect about what they say to the teacher, in their efforts, perhaps, to gain approval. The range of communicated information is wide in any given classroom.

Having parents in the classroom offers an opportunity to learn about their style with their children.

> In an Early Head Start classroom, one- and two-year-olds arrive with their parents. The program's practice is to offer breakfast (fruit, cereal, juice, pancakes), allow the children to eat what they choose, and then get up to play. The teachers bring them to the table. The parents of several of the Chinese children sit down with them, open containers they have brought from home, holding congee (a traditional rice cereal), noodles, or meat-filled buns. The parents feed the children by spooning the food into their mouths. The children eat a few bites, then wander off to play. Lia's mom follows her around the room, spooning congee into her mouth every time Lia pauses. Jeffrey's dad keeps him sitting at the table, scolding him, by saying, "You have to eat!" Ann's mother stays in the hall, feeding Ann on her lap, unwilling to come into the classroom because it will distract Ann from eating.
>
> (C. Barclay, final essay for master's degree, 2003)

PARENTS CONTRIBUTE TO CHILDREN'S SECURITY

As pointed out in Chapter 2, studies of parent-child attachment are not new. Years ago, research showed that children are more exploratory and more openly social in an unfamiliar environment if they are accompanied by a familiar adult, usually a parent (Arsenian, 1943; Cox & Campbell, 1968; Rheingold & Eckerman, 1971). However, these children behaved quite differently in the same strange environment when their parents were not there. Rather than investigating the objects in the environment and exploring the space, some children showed distress by crying, thumb-sucking, or stamping their feet. Others spoke less, stopped playing, or moved about hesitantly. With the familiar adult present, the children played, spoke, and moved about comfortably. Apparently the adults' presence was a secure base from which the children could wander, explore, and return. These and more recent studies have been interpreted to mean that the adults' presence communicated a feeling of power to the children, while the adults' absence conveyed powerlessness (Caruso, 1989; Howes, 1988; Karen, 1994; Raikes, 1996; Schore, 2001).

You can probably translate these research findings into your own life. Have you ever had the feeling, when embarking alone on a new adventure, that you would rather have the company of a familiar person? Is it more comfortable for you to walk into a room full of strangers with another, known person than by yourself? Do you remember going to college and feeling that you would like to have one of your family members or a close friend with you, at least for a short time? Did you ever wish for the comfort of your old home after you moved to a new location? These natural longings for familiarity in new and untried situations are a part of our human heritage.

Though young children feel safer with their parents nearby, they also have a great push from within to steer their own ship. "You're not the boss of me!" the 4-year-old cries out against adult authority. "I do it myself!" the 2-year-old shouts at offers of help. These conflicting tides are unsettling to children as well as to adults. While one urge pulls the child toward adult protection, the other propels the child away into a sea of her own actions. Even we, as adults, may experience conflicting feelings—wanting and simultaneously not wanting to be separate, independent, and autonomous; wanting and at the same time not wanting to be connected to or merged with another person.

TEACHERS ALSO EXPERIENCE CONFLICT

Is it any surprise that when children enter a program, torn between wanting to leave their parents and wanting to hold on to them, that teachers, too, get caught up in the age-old dilemma? "The maturing adult is continually reliving and revising his memories of childhood, redefining his identity, reforging the shape of his selfhood, discovering new facets of his being" (Kaplan, 1978, p. 32). This conflict between wanting to be autonomous and wanting to be dependent exists to some degree in all adults. Surely you have felt that pull between the feeling that "I'd just like to go to bed, pull the covers over my head, and forget everything" and the feeling that "I can take care of it." These adult feelings have some similarity to the contrary pulls that children experience, especially when they enter school.

Recognition of this conflict is the important and necessary first step for teachers. Young children and parents need help resolving this conflict when children begin school. It is a heavy burden that falls on the teacher's shoulders.

While young children need their parents to help them make a comfortable transition from home to school or center, teachers often wish this were not so. "If only those parents would get out of the room, I could get on with my work with the children." How often we hear that said! Sometimes program rules serve this purpose.

Children are to ride the bus on the first day. Seats are for children only.

Parents bringing children on the first day may stay for the first half hour.

Such regulations send strong messages to parents that they are not wanted.

Yet parents have feelings about their children's first days at a program that need to be recognized and supported by teachers. Parents also need to have control over their children's lives and to have a say in how their children will make the transition from home to school. Rules that keep them out deny them this control, as do rules that dictate overly structured entry schedules. How to arrive at an entry procedure that meets the needs of each parent and child is truly challenging.

How teachers and parents work together in the first days will contribute to a spirit of either cooperation or competition. This teacher tried, with the best intentions, to make the parent feel comfortable, but the effort backfired:

Andrea greets 2-year-old Dario and his mother as they enter the Early Head Start room. He huddles behind her. She pulls him out to stand in front of her. "Say 'Good morning, Andrea.'" Dario tries to go behind her again. "You have to say 'Good morning, Andrea.'" Andrea says, "Good morning, Dario. How are you today? How are you, Ms. Phillips? Has it been a hard morning?" Andrea, seeing the rising tension between mother and child, tries to take the pressure off by saying, "It's OK. He doesn't have to say it if he doesn't feel like it." The mother, now even more agitated, almost yells, "Don't tell me how to raise my child!"

Learning from parents in the beginning days is not always easy. In order for the relationship to develop productively, this teacher now had to begin to gently mend the rift. When teachers and parents work as partners, they will discover the fine-tuning in their relationship that is needed to succeed in this endeavor. Getting together as a parent group can initiate this connecting process.

A PARENTS' MEETING BEFORE THE PROGRAM OPENS

In addition to an individual conference between a teacher and parents, a meeting for all the parents, held before the program starts, can ease the initial entry phase. This may be more difficult to accomplish in a child-care setting where children sometimes enter at various times throughout the year. It can be done, however, within 3 months of entry dates.

A meeting focusing on beginnings and the separation of parent and child validates for parents that this is an occasion meriting attention. Holding such a meeting in the evening makes it possible for a wider array of parents to attend. Providing refreshments and name tags helps to loosen the tensions people feel when they participate in a group consisting mainly of strangers. Though the teacher may be familiar with many who are attending, most of the parents probably will not know one another. One of the positive aspects of a meeting for parents is their making contact with other parents of young children, infants, and toddlers. Thus the meeting provides both a social and an educational function. As one parent said, "I liked having other parents who, as I gradually got to know them, I could learn from and talk with about the progress and process of being parents and raising children."

The meeting can have several different components. Inviting several "old" parents from the year before to speak about their experiences and feelings at the beginning of the year sets a tone of sharing and comfort. Displaying the work of children from past years—their paintings, drawings, clay work, wood constructions—lends a flavor encouraging the parents' positive anticipation. Quotes from preschool children indicating how they managed the entry process would be reassuring for new parents. Photographs, a video, or PowerPoint presentation of children and parents during entry days would help to make the process concrete and tangible. Parents of infants and toddlers would see little twosomes engaged together in the new environment. Suggestions of books to read to children about separation and entry might be a welcome aid for parents (see Appendix A for a list of recommended texts), as well as the criteria for choosing good books (see Chapter 4). Providing a book list as well as actual books for borrowing is a supportive action. It is helpful to tell parents to read these stories as they would read any stories, in a context that is relaxed and enjoyable.

The tone of the meeting takes shape mainly from the sort of person the leader is. A meeting led by a relaxed, informal person takes on those characteristics, whereas a meeting of a leader more comfortable with set structure will reflect these preferences. The prior experience of the group leader will also dictate how well the meeting goes. Perhaps the most important feature of the meeting will be the sharing parents do with one another. This meeting should *not* be a lecture. Meetings designed to encourage a maximum amount of group participation are considered one of the most effective techniques for adults (Berger, 1981). Such active group discussions provide the following benefits:

- They help those taking part to clarify their thinking, and to integrate their thoughts with those of others.
- Hearing the experiences of others gives parents some perspective on and help in solving many of their own problems.
- Parents gain a better understanding of their children and themselves through the discussion of common problems.
- Through participation in group thinking, parents not only acquire knowledge but often come to feel differently about things.

Group discussions are facilitated by the physical arrangement of people in the room. If parents are seated in a circle, they are most likely to talk to one another as they exchange ideas. Conversely, if they are seated in rows, they are more likely to address their remarks to the teacher who is leading the group, because they do not make eye contact with other parents as easily. The leader will need to decide which arrangement furthers the goal for the meeting.

Giving information about the beginning days may be an important aspect of this first meeting. Even though the program may have mailed out written information about the entry procedure (see Appendix B for a sample), it would be good to discuss the policy with parents. This provides an opportunity for them to raise questions and concerns about procedure. It also opens up the topic of separation and encourages parents to express their feelings about leaving their children.

In one such parents' meeting, a father of a 1-year-old asked, "How does it go for parents when you say goodbye at the center as opposed to saying goodbye at home?" He seemed worried that his daughter might have different feelings about being left at home with a babysitter than being left at the center. Or, possibly, this father was really talking about his own feelings.

The teacher in this case was very experienced with school beginnings and gave a long, explicit answer:

> Everyone has a different way of saying goodbye. You and I can talk about how you say goodbye at your house, and I can learn from you. There's no set answer about how we say goodbye here, but we do ask you to say goodbye. What we want is to make links with home before you say goodbye here. You'll provide pictures of yourselves to hang on our wall. I will send a letter to the children telling them that I am waiting to see them. You'll be talking with the children at home about the center. You'll be teaching us about your children. We have already learned that Katherine is called Katie; that George carries the corner of an old blanket to every new place. We also make home visits. We get to know that

your cat is black, where the kitchen is, what's your child's favorite plaything.

We'll ask you to stay close to the building when you first say goodbye, and we'll ask you to come back soon. Everyone will be on an individual schedule. It's not step by step. It's a process; it goes on all year. There will be give and take between the teachers and the parents.

We are fortunate to have a wide array of families: single parent families, two parent families; bilingual families; adoptive families, gay and lesbian families; bicultural families; families of color. We welcome you all and look forward to working with you over the year.

The teacher's answer seemed reassuring to many of the parents, and they felt free to begin asking questions. Since this was an all-day program for infants and toddlers, people asked questions about naps, about the various activities in which the children would be involved, about schedules eating, playing, going outdoors, and sleeping. There was concern about going-home time: "Do all the children think it's time to go when the first child is picked up?"

The teacher did not immediately answer all questions directly. Often she encouraged other parents to give an opinion if it seemed appropriate, or she asked parents to raise other, related questions, and then she answered them together. In that way parents began to share their concerns with one another. They found out that they were not alone in their worries.

Here are some of the questions parents wanted to discuss:

How long will it take before my son can stay without me?

What do you do if a child cries a lot?

My daughter is used to my leaving for work. Can my sitter bring her here?

If my baby needs a morning nap, and the other children are going outdoors, who will stay with her?

What do you do if my child gets sick? Or hurt?

My boy has never been left with anyone outside the family. How long will it take for him to get used to the center?

Will I be able to come in during the day to nurse her?

Will there be an opportunity for me to tell you some things about her eating preferences and habits?

I am a grandmother raising my grandchild; how will the other children react to me? What will you say if they ask where his mother is?

The answers provided to parents will depend on the design for beginnings that the program has developed. A plan that includes the following features will reassure parents and support children's positive growth and development:

- A home visit
- A gradual and staggered entry
- A slow-paced phasing-in period that includes parents
- An individual approach to each parent-child style of separating
- A time and place for parent conferences or miniconferences
- A general belief in the importance of this separation event

There is a good chance that both children and parents will emerge from this experience feeling that they have been cared for and nurtured at a time when they need it most. It is easier for parents to cope with a difficult situation when they feel supported and encouraged.

FATHERS AND CHILDREN

Not all conferences and parental contact are with mothers. While the word "parent" is still largely equated with mothers in this society, it is a growing reality that many men are deeply involved in the day-to-day care of their children. There are those who share child care with women or male partners, and those who have sole responsibility for the rearing of their children. Teachers' own attitudes toward men as nurturers will partially develop from the amount of experience they have had with men as caretakers of young children.

During the past 2 decades the role of the father has been changing profoundly. Many men are exploring new ways to express both their masculinity and nurturance, a combination that has not existed traditionally in this country. As one father wrote: "One of the most significant changes in fathering today is the recognition that fathers need not be bound by the traditional roles handed down by their fathers and grandfathers. . . . They want to balance and integrate the provider/protector role with the nurturer/caregiver role" (Franklin, 1983, p. 9).

This shift in role has produced conflict for many men, and they often experience ambivalence about the meaning of masculinity. At the same time, both men and women have mixed feelings about men who are taking on a new role. Caretaking men in some cultures are regarded as less than masculine or their work is viewed as unimportant.

Many men are deeply involved in the day-to-day care of their children.

A significant finding from studies of fathers is that children are more attached to fathers than had previously been acknowledged. Fathers have been shown to find school separations stressful (Bloom-Feshbach, Bloom-Feshbach, & Gaughran, 1980; Hock, McKenry, Hock, Triolo, & Stewart, 1980). The implications for teachers are obvious. Fathers need as much empathy and attention during the separation process as do mothers and children, and fathers can be effective in helping children adjust to the new situation.

> Marcus, age 4, stood outside the classroom door, refusing to come in, burying his face and body in his father's legs. The teacher encouraged them to enter, but short of dragging Marcus in, it was clearly impossible. The teacher left the door open and encouraged the father to stay there with Marcus, for the short first-day session. She repeatedly made contact with them, speaking encouraging words to the father in her attempt to help him find comfort in this uncomfortable situation.

The next day, the teacher and Marcus's father decided that he would carry Marcus into the room. Mr. Carr sat in a chair with Marcus on his lap. Marcus hid his face on his father's shoulder and closed his eyes, refusing to look at the room or the teacher who tried to play a peekaboo game with him. The teacher shared Mr. Carr's discouragement but urged him to continue to come to the classroom the next day.

When Mr. Carr arrived on Day 3, Marcus was willing to walk in with him and again sit on his lap. As long as Mr. Carr kept his arms around Marcus, he was willing to sit up and look around. Although the teacher smiled and spoke to them both many times during the shortened morning session, Marcus remained stony-faced and still. The teacher reminded Mr. Carr that progress had been made since the first morning and communicated her faith that eventually Marcus would let go of his father and come to school.

The next few days proved her right. Her continuing support of Mr. Carr and her reaching out to Marcus allowed him gradually to slip from lap to floor, from standing next to his father to sitting at a table with a puzzle, to painting, to engagement with the teacher, and finally to interacting with other children.

Mr. Carr and the teacher built a strong relationship in those first few days. While Mr. Carr continued to be an important person to Marcus, the boy finally was able to transfer some of his trust from his father to the teacher.

As recently as 20 years ago men were neglected in the child development literature (Lamb, 1981); few books for teachers included a point of view about fathers. Resources are now more available in publications by authors such as Lamb (1997), Levine and Pittinsky (1997), Pruett (2000), and Parke and Amin (1999), as well as on the Internet. However, with increasing numbers of men from various cultures becoming involved in the daily care of their children, as well as entering the early childhood profession, it is a matter of some urgency that teachers of young children think about the implications of this. Teachers must ask themselves:

- How comfortable are you in relating to fathers, both as they stay with their children in your classroom and as you hold conferences with them?
- Give some thought to your own child-rearing. How did you, as a child, regard the role of men in bringing up children? Can you identify any remains of those old feelings that shape your present attitudes?

- When a father, rather than a mother, picks up his son or daughter at the end of the day, is your behavior the same or different? If different, do you know in what way it is different? And why?
- What have been some of your successful communications with fathers? You may wish to make a list to share with your coworkers.

The absorption of fathers and men in the lives of young children is a trend gaining much momentum and is adding richness to the lives of all.

VARIED APPROACHES TO HELPING PARENTS

Sometimes the entry and separation procedure do not go smoothly. Some children and parents have a difficult time (see Chapter 3 for a description of a hard adjustment of a 3-month-old baby.)These difficulties take many forms, and while there may be elements of similarity from one relationship to the next, no two parent-child pairs are exactly alike in the way they cope. Because of this, there are various ways for teachers to help parents through this time—different things to say, different approaches to take.

Parents often look to the teacher to help them know what to do. A teacher may need to make decisions with several parent-child pairs and each may be unique.

> Gloria was clearly shocked and angry when her child screamed and cried as she attempted to leave her in the center. "I think she's pulling an act," Gloria told the teacher.
>
> "Why do you suspect that?" the teacher asked.
>
> "Well, she's never done anything like this before. She never cried or anything when l went to work and left her at her grandma's. And now that her grandma works, I have to bring her here."
>
> As the teacher and mother discussed Angela's behavior, Gloria revealed that she had never left 3-year-old Angela in any strange place before. Gloria, however, insisted it was an "act" and that Angela should straighten out and stay in school without such a big fuss. Besides, Gloria had to go to work and couldn't be spending long hours at the center.
>
> The teacher, recognizing Gloria's need to leave for work, supported her leaving, and reassured her that she would take good care of Angela.
>
> "Children frequently cry and cling to their mothers when they are left in a new place. They're frightened and worried about themselves. We understand that in this center, and we'll do every-

thing we can to help Angela feel safe. We'll hold her and play with her. Why don't you call us when you have a break at work and we'll tell you what's going on here. You can talk to Angela, too. She might cry when she hears your voice, so prepare yourself. What it means is that she loves you and misses you. But the phone call is important for her. It's a way of telling her that you're still OK and that you love her, and miss her, too, and you will be back."

Perhaps Gloria said that she did not expect Angela to behave that way because she was afraid that the teacher would not accept Angela into her center. On the other hand, perhaps she was genuinely surprised. Whatever the case, Gloria needed the teacher's help just as much as Angela did. Telling Gloria to phone when she got to work was a way of informing her that the teacher is on her side and that the teacher knows how worried she feels, even if she never said so.

Sometimes parents are angry at the teacher for suggesting that they stay with their child. They take it as an insult. This makes some teachers very defensive. Teachers sometimes feel that they are trying to make life "nice" for the child and the parents are giving them a hard time.

What should a teacher do? It seldom helps to get into a verbal battle with a parent at that point, especially when the child so clearly needs the parent to be there. This may occur despite the fact that the parent has received all the information about entry that other parents have. It is important for the teacher to be firm without being angry.

I can see that you're uncomfortable here with Nikki and that you'd prefer to leave. l can understand your feeling of wanting to go when she clings that way. But it's so common for children to act like that at this age—we pretty much expect it here. She truly seems to need you and isn't ready yet to accept me. Do you have any suggestions for how l might get to know Nikki—things that she particularly likes to do and could do with me so that she'll come to trust me and feel safe here?

The teacher has tried to enlist Nikki's mother in the solution of this problem and help her become responsible for the comfort of her own child. The teacher has set a tone of cooperation as well as empowerment for the parent.

If the parent insists on leaving, the teacher might also ask, "Who else takes care of her? Might that person be able to spend some time with her here?"

A teacher may notice a child who has some worries about staying in school and want to share that information with his or her parent. Often miniconferences, especially at pick-up time, seem to take place in a natural way. Here is how one teacher used those informal times in a positive way:

> I have had many miniconferences with Eyon's mother in which we both shared our concern about Eyon's reticence. Ms. Ross really tuned in during these conferences, and we did some good teamwork. A few times, Ms. Ross took Eyon out of the classroom at noon so that they could have lunch together and she could give Eyon more focused, intimate talking time. In the classroom, I tried to give Eyon the support and encouragement he needed, and he seems finally to be coming into his own. He seems to be feeling stronger about being Eyon, and I think he is ready to use language more abundantly.

Some parents need help in leaving the child: such as a mother who holds her child on her lap for long periods of time, or a father who leaves, then returns in a few minutes, leaves again but peers through the classroom window for a long time. It often relieves parents who seem so ambivalent if teachers are honest with them:

> You seem to be having trouble making up your mind about whether Alba should be here or not. A lot of parents feel that way—they want their children to have a good time in the center, but at the same time they feel unhappy about the fact that the children are growing up or spending time away from them. Would it help if you went out for half an hour or an hour and then came back? We could increase the time out of the room each day until you both feel comfortable. Why don't you tell me when you're ready to do that?

Some teachers provide a pot of coffee in the hall or in a nearby room for parents during these beginning days, to help them as they begin to take short leaves from the room.

Sometimes parents are concerned about leaving their children but do not share those feelings with the teacher. This might be because they themselves are shy or because they believe that the teacher may see them as interfering in the classroom life. If a teacher senses that a parent may need support, discussing the matter may help to clear the air.

> Rich often gave directions to his 10-month-old son, Simon, and to the caregivers as well. The caregiver felt that perhaps Rich needed reassurance that Simon was being looked after in the center. When

she asked him how he felt about leaving Simon with her, he told her that he felt a little apprehensive because Simon was so quiet and undemanding that sometimes he could be overlooked. The teacher assured Rich that she would take good care of Simon and that she was very fond of the baby. The teacher agreed with Rich that sometimes quiet children can, indeed, be overlooked.

Once in a while a teacher may find that after a suitable period of time a child is ready to move out on his or her own but the parent is not. Whether for cultural or personal reasons, it may be hard for the parent to say that final goodbye and leave the room. This frequently annoys teachers. Some empathy might provide a key:

It seems a little hard for you to say goodbye to Elysa. I wonder if we can make a plan to make it more comfortable for you.

Sometimes a little humor is needed to lighten the mood:

It looks like we've gotten Elysa settled, and now it seems as if we've got to help you settle, too! How can we go about it?

Teachers help young children and their parents to separate comfortably by communicating a sense of understanding and belief in their own ability to support the separation process. Parents' worries are lessened when they sense that teachers have faith that they will be able to care for the child competently and the parent is able to see that demonstrated daily. It is trying for parents to leave a sobbing child with the teacher, especially if it is the second or third month of the program. The teacher who recognizes that the separation process takes time and effort can share that with the parent through actions as well as words.

There is no way to foresee all the possible separation reactions that parents and children may experience and have suggestions for them all. Basically what happens between the teacher and the parents of the children will depend on how they view each other, and how they regard separation. The younger the child or baby, the more intense the parent's likely separation reactions, and the more flexible the teacher's response.

The teacher has assured Wendy that she can come into the room to feed her baby at any time. Wendy comes to the center every day on her lunch break to breast-feed her 7-month-old daughter. She quietly goes to Rosa's crib, picks her up, and sits in the nearby rocking chair with the still-sleeping baby. Wendy begins to rock and hum. She

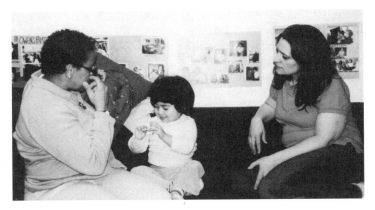

The teacher sits nearby as Ana plays with her mother, who will soon leave.

Her mother goes out the door.

The teacher and Ana wait by the window for her mother to appear on the street below.

There she is!

Ana reaches out—their hands almost touch.

Ana is comforted by her teacher's warm embrace.

strokes Rosa's nose with her finger until the baby stirs, opens her eyes, and gazes at her mother. "Hello, baby," she says softly as she opens her shirt and begins to nurse, "I miss you today, baby girl."

USING A QUESTIONNAIRE WITH PARENTS

In addition to talking with parents, teachers may wish to consider using a questionnaire focused on separation (see Figure 5.1). The answers parents provide may alert the teacher to possible reactions a child may have when leaving the parent becomes a reality. It is also designed to alert the parent to the possibility that his or her child may need attention and care when going through this particular event.

One advantage of a questionnaire is that it offers time for reflection— to the person answering, as well as to the person asking the questions. On the other hand, all the questions may not be suitable for all groups of parents. Furthermore, a questionnaire in English is not appropriate for parents with other native languages. A teacher can use the questionnaire as a guide for a conference with parents, going over only those questions that seem pertinent. If parents prefer to fill out the questionnaire on their own instead, a teacher might leave it with the parent at the time of the home visit, describing the kinds of questions it contains. Alternatively, a teacher might prefer to wait a few weeks, until teacher, parent, and child know each other better, to ask that a questionnaire be answered.

Since people react differently to questionnaires, it is important for parents to recognize that the answers they provide will help the teacher know his or her children better and improve his or her work with them.

Here are some questions teachers might ask themselves in evaluating the questionnaire for use:

- Will parents need help in understanding why I want to know some of these facts?
- Would it be best to fill out this questionnaire together with the parent? Would it be better to do it with both parents rather than one?
- Would the questionnaire provide a good basis for our conference?
- How can I make good use of the answers? What do the answers tell me about the child? About the parents?
- What shall I do with information that indicates the parents have a very different attitude from mine about child-rearing?

The sample questionnaire in Figure 5.1 is not a scientifically perfected instrument, nor is it meant to be. Rather, it is only a guide to help a teacher

FIGURE 5.1. Parent Questionnaire Focusing on Separation

---

1. How old was your child when you first left him or her with a relative, babysitter, or someone other than yourself?
   How did your child react at that time?
   How does your child react now?
   Have there been any changes in the people who take care of him or her?
   If yes, how did your child react to those changes?

2. How do you feel when you leave your child with another person for care?
   Do you use any special routines with him or her when you are leaving?

3. Does your child have a favorite blanket, toy, or object to which he or she is attached?
   Under what circumstances does your child use it?

4. How does your child react to people he or she does not know, either in or outside your home?

5. Has your child ever been left accidentally for a brief time, such as in the supermarket or a store? What was the child's reaction?

6. How does your child behave when faced with a new group, such as a birthday party or a family gathering?

7. Has your child ever stayed overnight at the home of a friend or relative? If yes, describe his or her reactions to the experience.

8. Have either or both parents been away from the child overnight or for a period of time?
   If yes, how old was the child at the time?
   How did he or she react to this separation?
   Who cared for your child at that time?

9. Has your child ever been hospitalized?
   If yes, at what age?
   For what reason?
   For what length of time?
   Were parents able to stay with the child?
   Describe the circumstances, including your child's reactions to this hospitalization.
   How did your child behave when he or she came home?

(*continued*)

FIGURE 5.1. (continued)

10. Was either parent ever hospitalized?
    For what length of time?
    What was the child told?
    Was the child permitted to visit?
    What were his or her reactions?

11. Has there been a death of anyone close to your family, or of a pet?
    If yes, what was the child's relationship to that person?
    What was the child told?
    What were his or her reactions to the death?

12. If you and your spouse or partner have been separated or divorced, what is
    the living arrangement for your child?
    What has been the child's reaction to this situation?
    In what way do you think it will affect your child's entry into this program
    and his or her separation from you?

13. Have you moved during the child's lifetime?
    If yes, how many times?
    How old was your child?
    How did he or she react to the move?

14. What does your child do when he or she is angry? Afraid? Sad? Happy?

15. What makes your child fearful?

16. What helps your child recover from emotional stress?

17. How do you think your child will react to starting early care and education?
    How do you think your child will react when you leave him or her here
    without you?

18. Is your child comfortable taking a nap alone on a cot or crib?

19. What does your child like to do that may help us plan activities for him
    or her?

20. What are your child's favorite games? Storybooks? Toys?

21. What else would you like us to know about your child that would help us
    in planning for a most comfortable entry into our program and the most
    comfortable separation for both of you?

Note: This questionnaire is based, in part, on the "Parental Anxiety Rating Scale," reported in the
work of Doris, McIntyre, Kelsey, and Lehman (1971).

and parents focus on some aspect of a child's experiences and personality that may relate to the entry and separation process. Its purpose is to sensitize adults to the meaning of children's behaviors at this time.

As infants, toddlers, and young children enter early care and education for the first time, the work that teachers and parents do together makes an impact on the transition. This chapter has highlighted the support that parents and teachers need from each other in their efforts to help children achieve the shift from home to school or center with a minimum amount of stress.

6

Entry and Separation Policy

ALL EARLY CARE AND EDUCATION settings have a point of view about the entry and separation process, whether they ignore it or make plans for it. If they ignore it, then most likely their point of view is based on a conventional stance that separation is not an event of special importance and that to drop a child and run is best for everyone concerned. If there is a plan for entry and separation, then this is an acknowledgment that parent-child attachment is significant. There are many degrees of this acknowledgment. They range from requiring a parent to stay with a child the first day to making ongoing individual plans to meet the needs of each parent-child pair.

This book reflects the position that adult-child attachment is a basic *necessity* for healthy human development. Without the security of this attachment, children are limited in their capacity to become related human beings, capable of conceptual and creative activity. Helping children achieve a successful separation and adjustment to early care and education settings is an incomparable opportunity for teachers and parents to support young children's development. When children are able to master their separation feelings at school or childcare entry, they achieve a giant step in their growth. This separation becomes "a healthy prototype for all the separations that will follow" (Furman, 1972, p. 234).

When a program regards entry and separation as an opportunity for growth, rather than a problem, its policies will support this idea. Teachers who believe in the effectiveness of their work concerning separation will be more supported and encouraged in schools or centers whose policies are consonant with their ideas. When a program's policy, for example, includes a parents' meeting during the phase-in period, as described in Chapter 5, families know that they have been respected and seriously included in the plans for the phase-in period of the program. Following are some other policies that identify entry and the separation process as growth and development opportunities for children.

INFORMATION FOR PARENTS AND
A WELCOME LETTER FOR CHILDREN

Many early care and education programs send information to families containing a short description of, and explanation for, opening activities. Look in Appendix B for a sample letter that describes a program's philosophy about separation, attachment, and beginning days. This written communication introduces parents to classroom "hellos and goodbyes" during the first early weeks.

Enclosed with the letter to parents is a teacher or caregiver's note for the child or the baby:

> Dear Wayne:
>
> Soon your mom (dad, grandma, aunt, uncle, etc.) will be bringing you to my classroom. We have so many wonderful toys and games for you to play with. When l see you, l will say, "Hello, Wayne! I'm so glad to see you here. I've been waiting for you."
>
> Your teacher,

A SPECIAL "SPRUCE-UP" TIME

School policy might entail a "room spruce-up" in which new children and their families participate along with "old" children and families. While such an event is well-suited to parent co-ops and programs that have a specific fall opening, it can be adapted to ongoing programs as well. Set aside a weekend morning or an evening to accommodate all those who wish to participate. In an ongoing program, evening is obviously best. Such a "work day/night" is not only a genuine help for the classroom, but a social "icebreaker" to boot. Teachers, parents, and children work together sorting out broken playthings, washing or painting pieces of equipment (using washable paint) refreshing tables and chairs, or performing other maintenance tasks. If a family member is adept at carpentry, he or she might be willing to build a loft or other desired addition. The work runs most smoothly when the teacher prepares a list of chores, specified for adults or children, and provides needed supplies. Don't forget that toddlers and young children love to wash tables and chairs. This "spruce-up time" offers an opportunity for both children and parents to become familiar with the classroom, feel a sense of belonging, and begin to know each other.

A FIRST VISIT

Can a program consider closing for a day in the spring to allow visits from children and parents who anticipate entering in the fall? This gives children a taste of the fun that is to come and provides a familiar reference point when they arrive for their first day. It enables parents to talk about the program with their children. Parents, too, enjoy feeling familiar with a new situation. A third advantage of this plan is that it is less disturbing to the ongoing class than a continual stream of visiting parents and children. Alternatively, visits for newcomers can be made immediately prior to the official opening day. This allows an informal, relaxed approach to the new setting and new teachers. When such a visit was not possible for one center, a particular family took their entering child to see the building where she would soon be attending child care.

Here is how some kindergartners were helped toward a smooth entry. In August, the school administrative district sent the following notice to parents of 5-year-olds, along with the bus schedule for the coming year:

> *Kindergarten*: On Tuesday, September 1, each kindergarten teacher will be in the classroom from 1:00 to 3:00 p.m. Parents are invited to bring their sons or daughters to meet their teacher. There will also be a school bus and driver at the school during the same hours for your children's familiarization.

Year-round early childhood programs need to create other arrangements for incoming children and families who frequently enter at varied times. Children can be brought for a first short stay either by a parent or the person who has been caring for them at home. Many programs find that a slow start, with the gradual addition of time spent in the room, over a period of a few days, increases the comfort of children and the security of parents. In most cases, this gradual entry leads to a successful adjustment.

One infant/toddler program makes an appointment with each parent and baby to visit the center before their starting day. They become acquainted with the room and the caregivers. Parents choose a crib (for the infant), and toddlers pick out a cubby for clothing and belongings. The caregiver puts their name and a small animal sticker on the cubby. "It says XAVIER right here, next to the cow."

These visits extend, but do not replace, the initial visits that parents must make on their own when they are searching for an appropriate early care and education setting.

HOME VISITS

Home visits, which are detailed in Chapter 5, can be part of a program's policy, provided that parents understand that they have the option to say no. Some parents do not feel comfortable about a teacher's visit. A parent might worry that the teacher may reject the child if he or she does not behave properly. As a substitute, the visit may take place in a nearby park or snack shop. Others welcome the visit as an opportunity to share a child's home life with the teacher. Likewise, some teachers may feel uncomfortable about such visits and need to be able to say no or, for support, take another staff member along. While some home visits occur before a program opens, others are arranged after the program has been in session when teacher and parents are better acquainted. A variation: one teacher took small groups of children, throughout the year, to each of the children's homes for juice and a snack by prearrangement with parents. All the children's homes were visited, and working parents were able to plan in advance to be present.

Most children love to have their teachers visit and often talk about it even at the end of the year.

A SLOW BEGINNING

To aid in the entry process, early care and education programs frequently offer short starting hours that are gradually lengthened during the first week or two of the program. (See Appendix B for an example of gradual plans.) In establishing a schedule for gradual entry, it may be that returning children generally require less time to settle in than first-time children do. Entry plans should take into account a child's previous experience. If he or she has been in group care before, what was the nature of that separation? Has she been home with a substitute caretaker? Does he have experience in activities outside the home?

All infants, toddlers, and their parents require a gradual entry. Allow several days and slowly lengthening time for a baby to adapt to the new setting, new caregivers, and new routine. Parents, too, need the gradual entry because mourning the loss of a young baby in out-of-home care is to be expected. In addition, parents need emotional support because the phase-in system imposes stressful impediments to their work schedules. No wonder they often leave in tears.

Twelve-month-old Sam's mother switched to center care because she had left him, unsatisfactorily, with various babysitters. He cried constantly when she went to work. Made aware of this, Rose, his primary caregiver at the center, helped the mother to phase in the baby gradually, each day a little longer stay without mom. The mother had to cut some of her work hours to manage this. Even so, the baby cried a lot. Because he refused to nap in his crib, Rose walked him in a stroller each day until he fell asleep. Eventually, the mother and Rose worked out a scheme together so he would nap in the crib.

In an ongoing program most likely there is a core of children who continue to be present when new children arrive. Often the "old" children offer help to newcomers. They invite them to play or share interesting toys, which are aids to, rather than substitutes for, a caregiver's help. Sometimes they contribute genuine affection when a newcomer succumbs to tears. Surely you've seen a toddler bring the right pacifier or special transitional object to a crying baby whose parent has just left. New children will usually look to their primary caregiver, however, for the major part of their security as they settle in, especially since their parents will be gone for long hours and may have limited time to spend at the center.

A plan for a slow beginning for infants and toddlers is a staggered entry in which each half of the group comes for part of the day. Because the room is less crowded parents, children, and teachers have more intimate access to one another. Appendix B includes an example of a staggered-entry plan.

ADJUSTMENT TO EATING AND SLEEPING

If the program includes lunch and a nap for very young children, these activities are often best added one at a time. Because sleeping and eating are potent reminders of home to young children, feelings are often strongly aroused at those times. If parents accompany children when they eat for the first few times and as they nap in the beginning, it eases children's anxiety. Children are often afraid to sleep in an unfamiliar setting. Perhaps they are reluctant to relinquish the control they have while they are awake. Many children need to feel very safe before they give up that control and fall asleep. Sleep is another separation. It is a transition from the wide-awake world to the passive world of slumber. In addition, many children live in cultures that value interdependence over independence and are not accustomed to sleeping alone. They need extra soothing and comfort at naptime.

A policy that acknowledges the special nature of food and sleep in the life of young children will do much toward facilitating their growth toward independent functioning in group care.

PARENTS IN THE CLASSROOM

When phase-in policy requires that parents stay with their children during the beginning days, parents, children, and teachers can jointly attend to the work of separating. Such a policy attaches dignity and importance to entry and adjustment and resolves for parents any ambivalence they might have about whether or not they should stay. Other actions support this policy, such as providing adult-sized chairs in the classroom and a pot of coffee in the hall or in a separate room for parents as they begin to leave the classroom for short intervals. When there is no choice about staying, parents should be informed of this policy before enrolling their child.

Other policy issues will arise. Should the parents sit with their children in the activity areas or around the periphery of the room? What will the teacher and a parent say to a child when the parent is about to leave the room?

When a teacher and parent agree that it is time to leave, it is important for a teacher to tell a child, "Your mom is leaving now. She will be back right after we finish reading a story," or "Your dad is going now. When you wake up from your nap he will come back to take you home." Then, as the parent says goodbye, suppose the child wants to go with the parent? If this is a part-time program and the parent is going to another room for coffee, it is reassuring for the child to see where that room is and to know that she can go there when she feels the need. On the other hand, if the parent is going to work and it is not possible for the child to go, then honesty is crucial. The teacher can say,"I know you'd like to leave with your mom, but she's going to work now and I will take good care of you while she's gone. She'll be back after our afternoon snack, you can depend on that. Moms always come back."

How will teachers arrange their time so that they can observe parent-child interactions and also be supportive to parents when they are in need? This is never easy to accomplish—it is a juggling act. Nevertheless, it is worth trying to figure out a way to perform both functions.

"SNEAKING OUT"

What about the parent who "sneaks out," or wishes to, when his or her child is engaged in some activity? Often teachers comply with this request. Why? I suspect that it relieves both parent and teacher of the responsibility for saying goodbye. Often it is easier to avoid a problem than to face it. All of us, at times, harbor a bit of the "coward" within us. Yet in most cases when parents disappear without telling children, they usually sense a parent's absence quickly. How do children feel when they believe that a protecting parent is nearby, only to discover that he or she is suddenly missing? Abandoned? Fearful? Untrusting? These feelings are hardly a firm foundation on which to begin a new experience. Consider the impact of this situation on a child's perception of a parent and on the child's perception of a teacher who has allowed this to happen. It must appear to children as deception rather than as trust. Should this happen without a teacher's knowledge, it is important to bring a parent back into the room and explain, outside of the child's presence, the problems with this practice.

As an adult you can probably understand children's feelings. For example, if a dentist told you he would be pulling a tooth, you would probably prepare yourself. If he started to pull it without telling you, you might be even more fearful. In addition, you might feel deceived. When you are told the truth, you are able to mobilize yourself to deal with the situation, no matter how difficult. In the coping you gain self-esteem.

It is similar for children. Having to deal with a painful event, and conquering it, brings gratification. When a child and parent say goodbye, the child and perhaps the parent may suffer some pain. The child who then struggles to overcome the pain, who finally, with the teacher's support, adjusts, takes a giant step toward self-confidence, self-reliance, and trust, and gains a large measure of self-control. When a parent sneaks out, however, his or her child is denied the opportunity to achieve such control.

SECURITY OBJECTS

Blankets, teddy bears, worn scraps of diapers, parents' handkerchiefs, nursing bottles, and such treasures are standard fare to which little children cling for safety. A policy that smiles on these transitional objects says, in effect, "We know how it is when you're very young and miss your family." It surely must feel comforting to young children when a teacher welcomes the stuffed animals and the blankets, allows children access to them at any time, and does not insist that they be shared.

Many other leave-taking rituals are reassuring to children. Some children have a special window or door from which to wave goodbye every day; others have a hug and kiss routine that never seems to vary; and still others insist that a parent read the same story day after day before leaving. Chapter 4 contains guidance for children who make the transition to a new teacher and classroom within the same building. Transitional objects and routines are very important in adding a solid base to the feeling of security.

AN END-OF-YEAR GET-TOGETHER

Just as policy acknowledges the importance of separation from home, it must also acknowledge the importance of separation from teachers and other children at the end of the year or whenever a child leaves the program. Partings are significant events in the lives of all those who have been intimately connected to one another in a group. An infant/toddler program held a goodbye picnic in a local park when they closed for the summer. At a preschool, the children heading for fall kindergarten sang a few songs and served their own baked cookies at an event for parents.

If your center is one that operates year-round and there is no formal ending day, a policy can be evolved that requires some form of recognition of individual children's last day. A classroom party or a special lunch to which the departing child's parents are invited is appropriate. Perhaps a picnic supper or a Saturday party could be arranged to mark the occasion. Make a "goodbye" booklet for departing children about their days in your program. Include photos of the child with friends and teachers engaged in favorite activities. Include drawings by friends. The booklet will be a treasured object that helps to bring closure. If one of the teachers also happens to be leaving, he or she can make a goodbye book to be left in the classroom.

Ceremonies like these help adults and children say goodbye before they go on to something new.

WHAT ABOUT A POLICY FOR CHILDREN
WHO ARE NOT READY?

A final consideration is for children who demonstrate that they are not ready to leave home and enter into group life with other children. These children may be unable to engage themselves with materials or enter into activities; they may be unable to respond to comfort offered by teachers; they may be unable to respond joyfully to the events and people in the program. What policy will be set for such situations?

A policy that is flexible will serve parents and children best. The needs and feelings of the parent and child in question must be considered versus the needs of the group and the teacher's own capabilities. Parents, teacher, and director, consulting together, will have to assess the child's potential for growth and make the most professional judgment possible, since there is no sure scientific measure available. Perhaps the most valuable contribution the teacher can make to the family in question will be to ensure that they not feel defeated or rejected. They need to feel supported and encouraged to believe that development of children takes time and that some children take longer than others. If the situation is extreme, referral to psychological counseling may be indicated.

THERE ARE GOOD AND BAD SEPARATIONS

Teachers need to be aware of the impact of their actions on young children when they leave their families for early care and education. Here are two contrasting observations that need no other commentary than themselves.

> Maritza, 32 months, arrives at the center for her second day, with her mother and grandmother. Her mother says (in Spanish) that she has to go and will see her after work. Maritza kisses her mother, smiles, and reaches for her grandmother's hand. Her grandmother leads her to the group of children and says (in Spanish), "Look at all the children, it is time to sit down." Maritza sits down, looks at her teacher, and smiles. Her grandmother says it is time for her to go, walks out of the classroom and shuts the door. Immediately, Maritza jumps up, begins to scream *"Abuela! Abuela!"* ("grandma"), and runs to the door. The other teacher grabs her by the arm, saying (in English), "No. You need to sit down!" Maritza continues to struggle to get free, screaming hysterically, *"Abuela!"*, and throwing her body in the direction of the door. The teacher continues tightly gripping Maritza's wrist, saying sternly "You need to sit down."

> Even though this is his third week in care, Derrick, almost 3 years old, enters the classroom with his father, who has been gradually leaving earlier each day. Derrick is crying softly and pulling at this father's pant leg. The teacher greets him, "Oh, Derrick, good morning." His father kisses him and says, "I'm leaving now." Derrick desperately grabs his pant leg, screaming, "No! No!" as his father goes out the door. Derrick kicks the door, hangs on the doorknob, screaming and crying, and begins to throw himself at the door and bang it with both hands. The teacher bends down and says, "I know you're sad and angry. You're sad because daddy left. But we will see daddy later. Daddy always comes back." As she is speaking, he stops screaming and looks at her. "Can I show you this fishy?" She holds out a book with a squishy plastic fish on the cover. Derrick looks away, moving closer to the door, and begins to kick and scream again. The teacher says, "Derrick, I know you're angry because daddy left." He takes the book, throws it on the

With our help children can evolve confident, competent, and self-assured.

floor, and pushes over a small wooden chair. "Derrick,"she says gently, "you're angry, but it is not okay to throw the chair. I'm going to help you fix the chair, and then I will help you find something else to play with." With her hand on his, they pick up the chair together. Though he has stopped crying, he continues to whimper. They walk over to the rug area where other children are playing with blocks and animals. She hands Derrick two different plastic animals. He chooses the dinosaur and sits down in the teacher's lap.

THE VALUE OF A SCHOOL POLICY
THAT SUPPORTS SEPARATION

It would be wonderful if all separations could be like this one with Caroline:

Caroline is standing with her back to her mother and the door, staring off into space. Hearing her mom's goodbye, she quickly turns and hugs her leg. Caroline's mom stoops down and Caroline climbs into her lap. "I don't want you to go," Caroline says in a quiet voice, peering intently into her mother's face. Her mom whispers in her ear, and Caroline cheerily replies, "OK. Have a good day." The mom stands up, and Caroline slides quickly behind her back, doing a peekaboo movement as she breaks into a giggle. Her mom tells her that she has to go. Caroline asks earnestly, "What time are you coming?" Her mom reassuringly answers, "Five o'clock on the dot—after your afternoon snack." Her mom leaves, and Caroline trots over to the easel.

However, since we know that there are many variations on this theme, we cannot expect that it will be like this for all children. Parents and teachers have a wonderful opportunity to contribute to the growth of the children entering early care and education and to help them become truly self-reliant. Self-reliance in the fullest sense is based on the knowledge that they are not alone but that "standing behind them, there are one or more trusted persons who will come to their aid should difficulties arise." The mark of the truly self-reliant person is "a capacity to rely trustingly on others when occasion demands and to know on whom it is appropriate to rely" (Bowlby, 1973, p. 359).

In an early care and education program where policy and practice value and support separation and attachment, more children will evolve as Caroline did—confident, competent, and self-assured.

Appendix A:
Suggested Reading

BOOKS FOR ADULTS

Baker, A. C., & Manfredi/Petitt, L. A. (2004). *Relationships, the heart of quality care: Creating community among adults in early care settings.* Washington, D.C.: National Association for the Education of Young Children.
> *The many ways in which relationships grow, develop, and make a difference in early care and education and how to sustain and nurture them.*

Bernstein, J. (1993). *Books to help children cope with separation and loss* (4th ed.). New York: R. R. Bowker.
> *In addition to a discussion of children's feelings about many kinds of separation and loss, this book gives guidelines for using books to help children cope. It also includes an extensive annotated bibliography of books for children through adolescence, plus a list of readings for adults.*

Bowlby, J. (1969). *Attachment and loss* (Vol. 1: *Attachment*). New York: Basic Books.

Bowlby, J. (1973). *Attachment and loss* (Vol.2: *Separation: Anxiety and anger*). New York: Basic Books.
> *The seminal work containing an extensive review of studies and writings on the nature of attachment and separation and an explanation of Bowlby's theory of the innate process of attachment.*

Bowlby, J. (1984). Attachment and loss: Retrospect and prospect. In S. Chess & A. Thomas (Eds.), *Annual progress in child psychiatry and child development: 1983* (pp. 29–47). New York: Brunner/Mazel.
> *An historical sketch and a clear explanation of Bowlby's theory of attachment, and the meaning of separation anxiety. Describes how he formulated his ideas based on observation of children.*

Brazelton, T. B., & Greenspan, S. I. (2000). *The irreducible needs of children: What every child must have to grow, learn, and flourish.* Cambridge, MA.: Perseus Publishing.
> *Two distinguished advocates for children, pediatrician Brazelton and psychiatrist Greenspan, lay out in clear terms what we need to do, as parents, teachers, and society, to ensure the future well-being of our children.*

Harwood, R. L., Miller, J. G., & Irizarry, N. L. (1995). *Culture and attachment: Perceptions of the child in context.* New York: The Guilford Press.

The authors explore how culture, specifically American and Puerto Rican, shape and influence the experience of parent-child attachment.

Honig, A. S. (2002). *Secure relationships: Nurturing infant/toddler attachment in early care settings.* Washington, D.C.: National Association for the Education of Young Children.

A thorough discussion of the needs for attachment for infants and toddlers who are in out-of-home care and how caregivers can make certain that these needs are met in child care.

Howes, C., & Ritchie, S. (2002). *A matter of trust: Connecting teachers and learners in the early childhood classroom.* New York: Teachers College Press.

Teachers who form secure attachments with the young children in their care create safe, competence-supporting, learning environments. Reviewing theory, research, and narratives from real classrooms, Howes and Ritchie provide teachers with many tools and resources from which to construct positive classroom communities.

Hyson, M. (2004). *The emotional development of young children: Building an emotion-centered curriculum* (2nd ed). New York: Teachers College Press.

Are children's emotions important? Not only important, but central to their social and intellectual development, as revealed in this book that is so full of supportive research and examples from everyday classrooms.

Kaplan, L. J. (1988). *Oneness and separateness: From infant to individual.* New York: Simon & Schuster. (Original work published 1978)

Describes and defines the infant's psychological journey from a state of unity with the mother to a state of being a separate and unique self. Provides the reader with an in-depth portrait of the developing young child.

Karen, R. (1994). *Becoming attached: Unfolding the mystery of the infant-mother bond and its impact on later life.* New York: Warner Books.

An examination of the history of attachment research, starting with Bowlby's seminal work onward, up to and including research conducted in the 70s and 80s. Dr. Karen's work helps us understand the depth and breadth meaning of parent-child attachment.

Lieberman, A. F. (1993). *The emotional life of the toddler.* New York: The Free Press.

A thoroughly sound, engaging, and in-depth look at children in the second and third years of life. Lieberman writes with coherence, understanding, and the ability to communicate important ideas to make our work with toddlers the best it can be.

National Research Council (U.S.). Committee on Integrating the Science of Early Childhood Development. (2000). *From neurons to neighborhoods: The science of early childhood development. Committee on Integrating the Science of Early Childhood Development; Jack P. Shonkoff and Deborah A. Phillips, editors.* Washington, D.C.: National Academy Press.

This book covers the whole range of early development and its context. According to the Acknowledgments it is "the product of a two-and-a-half-year project during which 17 individuals, as a committee, evaluated and integrated the current science of early childhood development" (p. ix).

Small, M. F. (1998). *Our babies, ourselves: How biology and culture shape the way we parent.* New York: Anchor Books.

> The culture of a family has a profound impact on its child-rearing decisions. This book reveals the many ways that babies are cared for and reared and helps readers understand how varied are the approaches to early care.

Viorst, J. (1986/1998). *Necessary losses: The loves, illusions, dependencies, and impossible expectations that all of us have to give up in order to grow.* New York: Simon & Schuster.

> Judith Viorst, author of many children's books, poetry, and other works, takes a long look at the many types of losses we experience all through life, beginning in childhood to the giving up of our own youth as we grow older.

BOOKS FOR CHILDREN

Alborough, J. (1999). *Hide and seek.* New York: Greenwillow Books.

> A flip-the-flap book. Frog is playing hide-and-seek with his friends, but he can't find anyone—until hippo jumps out and shouts boo! From then on the found animal joins the others, one after another, as they discover more and more friends.

Aliki (1996). *Hello, goodbye.* New York: Greenwillow Books.

> There are hellos and goodbyes in different languages and for many different situations, including a final goodbye that hurts the most and "lasts forever." The multicultural characters agree that the best goodbye is at bedtime, "when the sun goes down and the moon comes up."

Appelt, K. (2000). *Oh, my baby, little one.* New York: Harcourt, Inc.

> Mamma bird says goodbye to her baby in early care. Though she feels sad about leaving her baby, she carries love for her child throughout her day at work.

Brillhart, J. (2002). *Molly rides the school bus.* Chicago: Albert Whitman & Co.

> Molly is worried about riding the school bus on her first day of kindergarten, but a friendly older girl helps her adjust.

Brown, M. W. *Goodnight, moon.* (1947). New York: Harper & Row.

> In this classic story, a bunny ritually says goodnight to many objects in the bedroom, making the separation from the active daytime world into the dark, quiet sleeping world a comfortable transition. Bit by bit, the room gets darker as the bunny settles down to sleep.

Brown, M. W. *The runaway bunny.* (1972). New York: Harper & Row.

> The familiar story of a little bunny who wants to run away. Fortunately, his mother won't let him. Written in a repeated pattern, this is a reassuring story of a mother's love and stability.

Carlson, N. (2001). *Look out kindergarten, here I come!* New York: Viking.

> Henry, an enthusiastic gray mouse, is excited about starting kindergarten. He talks with his mother about all the fun he will have there. But when he actually gets to the school door, he bellows that he wants to go home. The teacher's warm encouragement turns the tide and he has a good day.

Christelow, E. (2004). *Five little monkeys play hide and seek.* New York: Hougton Mifflin/Clarion Books.

> It's bedtime. Lulu the babysitter comes and mama monkey goes out for the evening. Mama makes it clear that the five monkeys are to go to bed, and "no silliness." Then

the fun begins. They convince Lulu to count to ten as they hide. "Where are those monkeys? Where did they go? Where are they hiding? I really don't know." The games get more and more exciting, especially when mama comes home.

Cohen, M. (1989). *Will I have a friend?* (Rev ed.). New York: Collier.

A young child comes to preschool with his father and worries about finding a friend there. He does find one and his father says, "I thought you would."

Corey, D. (1999). *You go away* (2nd ed.). Chicago: Albert Whitman.

The simple text says, "You go away and you come back" in a variety of separation and reunion scenarios involving children, men, and women of different ethnic groups. A mother hides behind a blanket and then reappears; two children lose sight of their mother in the supermarket; a little girl goes to kindergarten.

Cummings, P. (1997). *My aunt came back.* New York: HarperCollins.

The well-traveled aunt goes to all sorts of exotic places and brings back fun things for her little niece. Told through outlandish rhymes and rhythms.

Danneberg, J. (2001). *First day jitters.* Watertown, MA: Charlesbridge Publishing.

Mr. Hartwell is trying to wake up Sarah. It's time to go to school, but she is hiding under the covers. She doesn't want to go to her new school. Finally, she dresses and gets in the car and at the end you discover that she's the teacher.

Downing, J. (2003). *Where is my mommy?* New York: HarperCollins.

A baby bunny and other animals wake up and ask, "Where is my mommy?" Each pair are eventually reunited. The story ends with a human child playing peekaboo with his mother, reinforcing the message that "Mommy always comes back."

Eastman, P. (1960). *Are you my mother?* New York: Designer Books/Random House, (*Eres tú mi mama?* New York: Random House, 1967.)

A little bird falls from the nest and asks everyone, and everything, including a steam shovel, "Are you my mother?" In the end, the two are joyously reunited in a surprising way.

Fowler, S. G. (1994). *I'll see you when the moon is full.* New York: Greenwillow Books.

Daddy is packing to go away on a trip. He and his little boy Abe tell each other how much they will miss one another. Daddy will be gone 2 weeks and will be back "when the moon is full."

Fox, M. (1993). *Time for bed.* San Diego, CA: Harcourt.

Rhymed couplets and lovely double-spread, oversized watercolors portray a variety of animals being lovingly tucked in for the night. Each animal has its own distinctive rhyme: "It's time for bed, little fish, little fish. So hold your breath and make a wish."

Gliori, D. (2001). *Flora's blanket.* New York: Orchard Books.

Flora, a little rabbit, cannot sleep without her missing blanket, so her whole family helps her look everywhere for it. Guess where it turns up?

Harris, R. (1978). *Don't forget to come back.* New York: Alfred Knopf.

Annie tries everything to prevent her parents from leaving for the evening. Their calm assurance when the sitter arrives and their own later return prove Annie's fear of abandonment groundless. A book to help spark a discussion of fears and feelings when being left.

Harris, R. (2003). *I am not going to school today!* New York: Margaret K. McElderry Books.

A little boy gets ready for the first day of school but soon decides he's not going. With the help of his parents and Hank the stuffed monkey, he gets there. Mr. Chase and Ms. Chen and a roomful of ethnically diverse children prove it to be a good day after all.

Henkes, K. (1993). *Owen.* New York: Greenwillow Books.

Owen, a small gray mouse, loves his old blankie, Fuzzy. Mom and dad wish he would give it up but none of their solutions work. Finally, mother cuts it up into handkerchief sizes and Owen is able to continue carrying it everywhere.

Henkes, K. (2000). *Wemberly worried.* New York: Greenwillow Books

A mouse named Wemberly who worries about everything, finds that she has a whole list of things to worry about when she faces the first day of school.

Hest, A. (1999). *Off to school, baby duck!* Cambridge, MA: Candlewick Press.

Baby duck was really scared and nervous about going to school. On his way there he meets Grampa, who is able to clear up some of his misconceptions, and baby duck is able to have a great day.

Hill, E. (1994). *Spot goes to school* (Rev ed.). New York: Puffin Books.

Spot is nervous about school, but he meets friends there and has a lot of fun. A lift-the-flap book.

Hill, E. (2003). *Where's Spot?* (Board ed.) New York: Putnam Publishing Group.

A very simple text and large illustrations make this a good choice for very young children. It is a hide-and-seek book about a playful dog.

Johnson, D. (1990). *What will mommy do when I'm at school?*

A little African-American girl who goes off to school for the first time is concerned about her mother's feelings. Maybe she'll be lonely or miss her little girl too much and be scared. Perhaps she'd better not go.

Joosse, B. M. (1991). *Mama do you love me?* San Francisco: Chronicle Books.

In a loving dialogue between an Inuit mother and her little daughter in Alaska, the daughter seeks assurance of her mother's love, and her mother never wavers in her declarations of love and commitment.

Kantrowitz, M. (1989). *Willy Bear* (Rev ed.). New York: Aladdin Paperbacks.

A little boy prepares himself for his first day at school by pretending that it is Willy Bear who will be going. He conquers his fear and bravely bids goodbye to Willy.

Katz, K. (2001). *Where is baby's mommy?* New York: Little Simon.

Lift the flaps to help baby find his mommy in this hide-and-seek game. "Is mommy behind the chair?" No she isn't, but finally he finds her.

Kaufmann, N. (2003) *Bye, bye!* Asheville, NC: Front Street.

All the animals are going to school with a parent, but when it comes time to say goodbye, little pig doesn't want his father to leave.

Keller, H. (1988). *Geraldine's blanket* (Rev ed.). New York: Harper Trophy.

A small pink pig adores her blanket and takes it everywhere. Mama and papa frown on this and can't figure out how to get rid of it. When Geraldine gets a new doll, she, herself, figures out a way to hold on to it that mama and papa approve.

Krauss, R. (1951). *The bundle book.* New York: Harper & Brothers.

An old favorite, in which a little girl plays a game of peekaboo with her mother, told with a tone of affection and fun.

Lionni, L. (1995). *Little Blue and Little Yellow.* New York: Harper Trophy.

This story is about two color daubs who are friends. When they hug one another, they become green. Then their parents don't recognize them! A happy reunion takes place when they return to their original blue and yellow colors.

McBratney, S. (1994). *Guess how much I love you.* Cambridge, MA: Candlewick Press.
A young bunny, Little Nutbrown Hare, tries to explain how much he loves his caregiver, Big Nutbrown Hare. Although each explanation is topped by the big bunny, in the end he reassures the little one that "I love you right up to the moon—and back."

McCarty, P. (1999). *Little bunny on the move.* New York: Henry Holt & Co.
A little bunny moves on resolutely through a variety of landscapes until he gets where he wants to go—back with all the other little bunnies in the meadow.

McGhee, A. (2002). *Countdown to kindergarten.* San Diego, CA: Silver Whistle/ Harcourt.
A little girl is going to kindergarten in 10 days and she's quite frantic about the rules she will encounter and obsessed about not being able to tie her shoes. As the day draws closer, she becomes even more worried and thinks she's "in big trouble." Once she gets there, however, the teacher is kind, the rules are not as she thought, and there are other children who can't tie their shoes, either.

McMullin, K. (1998). *If you were my bunny.* New York: Scholastic.
This is a lullaby that a mother sings to her child as if she were a few different animals. "If you were my puppy and I was your mama dog . . . I'd croon you a puppy lullaby." At the end we see the mother tucking in her little one.

Middleton, C. (2004). *Enrico starts school.* New York: Dial Books.
Five-year-old Enrico, a cat, sets off for school. After making many attempts to fit in with the others by acting in ways that don't win friends he decides, on the advice of an older child, just to be himself, and has a much better day.

Minchella, N. (2003). *Mamma will be home soon.* New York: Scholastic Press.
Lili spends a few days with her grandmother while her mother is away. She keeps thinking that she sees her mother's yellow hat everywhere she goes.

Ormerod, J. (1992a). *Come back kittens.* New York: Lothrop, Lee & Shepard.

Ormerod, J. (1992b). *Come back puppies.* New York: Lothrop, Lee & Shepard.
In these two books the animals run off and are lovingly urged to come back, which they do. The overlay pages, which hide and reveal the animals, provide a peekaboo experience for the reader.

Parr, T. (2002). *The daddy book.* Boston: Little, Brown & Co.
A simply told tale of what daddies do, from taking showers to making cookies, and how they love to hug and kiss their children.

Penn, A. (1993). *The kissing hand.* New York: The Child Welfare League of America.
When Chester the raccoon is reluctant to go to kindergarten for the first time, his mother teaches him a secret way to carry her love with him.

Rockwell, A. (2001). *Welcome to kindergarten.* New York: Walker & Co.
Tim and his mother visit the kindergarten he will be attending. He explores the different centers where he will paint, cook, and learn math and writing. He has such an enjoyable visit that he looks forward to starting very soon.

Rosenberry, V. (1999). *Vera's first day at school.* New York: Henry Holt.

Vera has a small mishap on her way to school and rather than being late, she goes back home. Her mother finds her hiding under the bed and gently takes her back to the classroom and a very welcoming teacher.

Rusackas, F. (2003). *I love you all day long.* New York: HarperCollins.
   Owen, a little pig, doesn't want to go to school but his mother reassures him that she loves him "all day long" while he is busy doing school activities.

Salzberg, B. (2002). *Peekaboo kisses.* New York: Red Wagon Books/Harcourt.
   Lift the flaps in this touch and feel book to find a series of playful animals who crave kisses. Each page is another animal that says "Peekaboo! I see soft duckling kisses."

Simmons, J. (1997). *Come along Daisy.* New York: Scholastic.
   Daisy doesn't obey her mother's admonition to stay close and goes off to play with other animals. She soon finds herself alone and frightened. After a short time, her mother finds her.

Slate, J., & Wolff, A. (2001). *Miss Bindergarten gets ready for kindergarten.* New York: Puffin Books.
   Miss Bindergarten, a lovely black and white dog, carefully prepares her classroom for her cherished students, as each of them—animals all—also get ready for the first day.

Steig, W. (1992). *Amos and Boris.* (Rev. ed.). New York: Farrar, Straus & Giroux.
   A mouse and a whale are the closest of friends. When they must separate, they never forget one another. A touchingly told story.

Tafuri, N. (1991). *Have you seen my duckling?* (Rev. ed.). New York: Harper Trophy.
   A mother duck asks other pond animals for help when she "loses" her eighth duckling who is really hidden out of (her) sight—but not the readers'.

Tafuri, N. (1998). *I love you, little one.* New York: Scholastic.
   A variety of animals ask, "Do you love me, mama?" Each loving mother gives a poetic and reassuring answer. Double-page, beautiful illustrations of mamas and babies speak of this love.

Tompert, A. (1992). *Will you come back for me?* (Rev. ed.). Chicago: Albert Whitman.
   Suki, an Asian child, is 4 years old. The family says it's time for Suki to go to a child-care center, so they go for a visit. The next day when Suki is to stay there, both she and her mother are sad when they part. So her mother reassures her that she will come back by making a big red paper heart—one half for each of them to hold.

Valens, A. (1990). *Jesse's Daycare.* Boston: Houghton Mifflin.
   When Jesse's mom goes to work, she brings Jesse to day care at Sarah's house. Both Jesse and his mom are busy all day in their separate places. At the end of the day they are happy to be together, telling one another what they've been doing.

Viorst, J. (1992). *The good-bye book.* (Rev. ed.). New York: Aladdin.
   The book begins, "Don't go. I don't want you to go. . . ." A little boy goes on to think of every outrageous reason for his parents to stay home. Indeed, they leave for the evening, but when the babysitter comes, the boy finally says goodbye.

Waddell, M. (1992). *Owl babies.* Cambridge, MA: Candlewick Press.
   Three little owls wonder where their mother is. The smallest owl cries out "I want my mommy!" After some tense moments, mother owl does return, much to everyone's relief.

Wells, R. (2004) *My kindergarten.* New York: Hyperion.
   Emily, the small rabbit, and her animal friends are in kindergarten for the first time.
   The story takes them month by month through a great variety of activities, play, and
   games plus the new things their teacher is teaching them. This is a long story and
   will be best for older five-year-olds.
Wells, R. (1995). *Edward unready for school.* New York: Dial Books.
   Edward, a shy young bear, was not ready for school. When he gets there he wants to
   go home. His teacher and parents agree that he's not ready yet, so they take him back
   home until he is ready.
Yolen, J. (2000). *How do dinosaurs say good night?* New York: Blue Sky/Scholastic.
   It's bedtime for dinosaur children, who happen to have human, multicultural par-
   ents. When papa (or mama) comes in to say goodnight, the question is "Does a dino-
   saur slam his tail and pout?" It turns out that the dinosaurs don't behave in any of
   those ways. They "give a big kiss" and go to bed.
Zolotow, C. (1998). *Wake up and goodnight.* New York: Harper Growing Tree.
   A very reassuring book about going to sleep and waking up. Read about waking up.
   Then flip the book over and read about going to sleep.

SELECTED PROFESSIONAL READINGS

Bernhardt, J. L. (2000). A primary caregiving system for infants and Toddlers: Best
   for everyone involved. *Young Children, 55*(2), 74–80.
Bove, C. (1999). Inserimento del bambino al nido (Welcoming the child into child
   care): Perspectives from Italy. *Young Children, 54*(2), 33–34.
Bromer, J. (1999). Cultural variations in child care: Values and actions. *Young
   Children, 54*(6), 72–78.
Chang, H. N.-L. with Pulido, D. (1994, October/November). The critical impor-
   tance of cultural and linguistic continuity for infants and toddlers. *Zero to
   Three,* 13–17.
Chang, H. N.-L. with Pulido, D. (2003). Culture and caregiving goals: Expectations
   & conflict. *Zero to Three, 23*(5), pp. 4–54.
Daniel, J. E. (1993). Infants to toddlers: Qualities of effective transitions. *Young
   Children, 48*(6), 16–21.
Elicker, J., & Fortner-Wood, C. (1995). Adult-child relationships in early childhood
   programs. *Young Children, 51*(1), 69–78.
Elliot, E. (2003). Helping a baby adjust to center care. *Young Children, 58*(4), 22–28.
Giovannini, D. (2001). Traces of childhood: A child's diary. In L. Gandini & C. P.
   Edwards (Eds.), *Bambini: The Italian approach to infant/toddler care.* New York:
   Teachers College Press.
Gonzalez-Mena, J. (2005). Attachment and separation. *Diversity in early care &
   education* (4th ed.) (Chapter 5, pp. 79–91). New York: McGraw-Hill.
Gonzalez-Mena, J., & Bhavnagri, N. P. (2000). Diversity and infant/toddler care-
   giving. *Young Children, 55*(5), 31–35.

Harkness, S., & Super, C. M. (Eds.). (1996). *Parents' cultural belief systems: Their origins, expressions and consequences.* New York: The Guilford Press.

Howes, C. (1998, June/July). Continuity of care: The importance of infant, toddler, caregiver relationships. *Zero to Three,* 7–11.

Johnston, L., & Mermin, J. (1994). Easing children's entry to school: Home visits help. *Young Children, 49*(5), 62–68.

Lee, F. Y. (1995, March). Asian parents as partners. *Young Children,* 4–9.

Lieberman, A. F. (1991, February 6–11) Attachment and exploration: The toddler's dilemma. *Zero to Three.* Download from www.zerotothree.org professional journal/classic articles #10.

New, R. (1999). Here we call it "Drop off and Pick up": Transition to child care American style. *Young Children, 54*(2), 34–35.

Pawl, J. H. (1990). Infants in day care: Reflections on experiences, expectations and relationships. *Zero to Three, 10*(3), 1–6. [Also available as a download, at www.ZerotoThree.org professional journal/classic article #8]

Raikes, H. (1996). A secure base for babies: Applying attachment concepts to the infant care setting. *Young Children, 51*(5), 59–67.

Szamreta, J. M. (2003). Peekaboo power to ease separation and build secure relationships. *Young Children, 58*(1), 88–94.

Whaley, K. L., & Kantor, R. (1992). Mixed-age grouping in infant/toddler child care: Enhancing developmental processes. *Child & Youth Care Forum, 21*(6), 369–385.

Appendix B:
Letter and Phase-In Schedules

SAMPLE LETTER TO PARENTS

Dear Parents:

Welcome! We look forward to a wonderful year with your children. We know the excitement (along with the uncertainty) that you may be feeling as your child's first day approaches.

Infants, toddlers, and young children exhibit a wide range of responses to their first days and weeks in care. For some children this will be their first experience separating from parents and caregivers. This is a big step, and individual children handle it differently from one another. There is no right or wrong way for children to behave during this transitional time.

While some children acclimate to new people and new situations quickly, others need more time. It is for this reason that we ask that a parent or caregiver remain in the building during the first days. While this may wreak havoc upon adult schedules, the rewards of a gradual beginning are substantial. Patience now will likely minimize separation struggles down the road. An important aspect of the separation process is consistency. Therefore, it is best if the same adult who will bring the child to school throughout the year be the one to participate during phase-in. Accompanying this letter is a phase-in schedule.

As every child (and parent) handles separation in his or her own way, *there will not be one strategy for everyone.* This may appear confusing at first, as we will be suggesting that some parent/caregivers say goodbye quickly, and asking others to stay in the room for a number of sessions. *All* accompanying adults will be asked to spend some time in the classroom during the first two or three sessions.

During phase-in, a staff room in the center will be available for parents and caregivers as they venture from the classroom for short periods of time. Sandra, the director, will serve as your eyes and ears during these brief separations to give "updates."

All parents and caregivers MUST say "goodbye" to their children. While it may be easier to sneak away while your child is happily engaged, this method can have tremendously negative implications. Imagine how disturbing it can be to look up, expecting to see your familiar adult nearby, and that adult has disappeared. It is important for a child to know what to expect, and to expect that the adults in his or her world are going to be clear about their comings and goings. Being honest about leaving will lend more credibility to the assurances you make to your child about returning.

In August, we will be calling you to arrange for a home visit. This visit is planned to allow children to have their teachers on their "territory." It also allows for teachers to acquire a fuller understanding of each child's experiences and interests and makes an important link between center and home.

Please bring the following items to the program:

- Several family photographs, including parents, siblings, caregivers, or any family members or friends with whom your child is close. Don't forget photos of pets! Please do not bring photos that you will want returned.
- Blanket, sheet, comfort item (stuffed animal, etc.) labeled.
- Notarized medical/trip release and health forms.
- Complete change of clothing labeled.
- Supply of diapers, labeled.
- Clear plastic storage box, labeled.

Once again, welcome to the new year at our program!

> Sincerely,
> Teachers of the Little Kids and the Big Kids

SAMPLE PHASE-IN SCHEDULES
FOR PARENTS AND CHILDREN

The Settling-In Period: Hello and Goodbye

For every child and parent, even those who are returning to our program, the first days are filled with new experiences, new people, and new expectations. We try to make this adjustment period as smooth and comfortable as it can be for each child and parent because we know that it sets the stage for a happy year and for future separations and transitions as well.

Each group will have a phase-in schedule, which gradually increases from an abbreviated day to the full program. Because we know how trying it is for parents to remain in the building or classroom for this beginning period, we will provide coffee and snacks in the office to help you along. Your child's teacher or caregiver will work closely with you after the first short scheduled days, to determine how, when, and for how long you will leave. Remember that goodbyes are different for each child-adult pair—what is right for one pair may not be right for another.

Preparing for the Phase-in

We know that you and your child have already paid a visit to our program. Now we suggest that you remind your child about the loving teacher who is waiting to help him/her play, learn, eat, and rest. This would be a good time to read a picture book from the attached list. It will reassure your young child that though you will say good-bye in the morning, you will *always* come back in the afternoon, and say hello!

The Settling-In Schedule

Phase-in for infants and toddlers

Please be prepared to remain with your child for the entire settling-in schedule.

WEEK ONE:
Children will come in half groups as follows:

Group 1:   Monday and Tuesday   8:30–9:45
           Wednesday and Thursday   8:30–10:00

(We ask Group 1 parents/caregivers to leave promptly at the scheduled time, so that teachers may prepare the classroom for Group 2)

Group 2:   Monday and Tuesday   10:15–11:30
           Wednesday and Thursday   10:15–11:45

Both groups 1 and 2:   Friday 8:30–11:00

WEEK TWO:
All children
Monday, Tuesday   8:30–12:00   Bring lunch
Wednesday, Thursday, Friday   8:30–2:00   Lunch and rest

WEEK THREE:
All children full schedule

Phase-in for twos and threes

WEEK ONE:
Monday, Tuesday, Wednesday	8:30–10:30	
Thursday, Friday	8:30–11:00	Bring snack

WEEK TWO:
Monday, Tuesday	8:30–12:00	Bring lunch
Wednesday, Thursday, Friday	Children come for full schedule, lunch, and rest.	

Phase-in for fours and fives

WEEK ONE:
Monday, Tuesday	8:30–12:00	Bring lunch
Wednesday, Thursday, Friday	8:30–2:00	Children stay for lunch and rest.

WEEK TWO:
All children come for full schedule.

Adjusting to Kindergarten

Parents and/or caregivers of kindergarten children who have never attended a prior program or who are feeling a little insecure may stay with the child for the first day until he or she feels safe in the classroom. In the instance of a child who is extremely anxious and cannot be comforted by the adult's presence, the teacher will be happy to arrange a conference with the parent in order to help the child have a successful entry.

References

Adams, S. A. (1995). *Homelessness and young children*. Unpublished masters thesis, Bank Street College of Education, New York.

Ainsworth, M.D.S., Bell, S. M., & Stayton, D. J. (1974). Infant-mother attachment and social development: "Socialization" as a product of reciprocal responsiveness to signals. In M. M. Richards (Ed.), *The integration of a child into a social world* (pp. 92–152). London: Cambridge University Press.

Ainsworth, M.D.S., & Wittig, B. A. (1969). Attachment and exploratory behavior of one year olds in a strange situation. In B. M. Foss (Ed.), *Determinants of infant behavior* (pp. 111–136). London: Methuen.

Albus, K. E., & Dozier, M. (1999). Indiscriminate friendliness and terror of strangers in infancy: Contributions from the study of infants in foster care. *Infant Mental Health Journal, 20*(1), 30–41.

Arsenian, J. M. (1943). Young children in an insecure situation. *The Journal of Abnormal and Social Psychology, 38*(2), 225–49.

Bell, S. (1970). The development of the concept of object as related to infant-mother attachment. *Child Development, 41*, 291–311.

Berger, E. H. (1981). *Parents as partners in education*. St. Louis: C. V. Mosby Co.

Bernhardt, J. L. (2000). A primary caregiving system for infants and toddlers: Best for everyone involved. *Young Children, 55*(2), 74–80.

Bloom-Feshbach, S., Bloom-Feshbach, J., & Gaughran, J. (1980). The child's tie to both parents: Separation and nursery school adjustment. *American Journal of Orthopsychiatry, 50*(3), 505–21.

Bowlby, J. (1969). *Attachment and loss* (Vol. 1: *Attachment*). New York: Basic Books.

Bowlby, J. (1973). *Attachment and loss* (Vol. 2: *Separation: Anxiety and anger*). New York: Basic Books.

Bowman, B. T. (1999). Kindergarten practices with children from low-income families. In Pianta, R. C., & Cox, M. J. (Eds). *The transition to kindergarten* (pp. 281–301). Baltimore: Paul Brookes.

Carey, B. (2004, June 29). Addicted to mother's love: It's biology, stupid. *New York Times*, p. F7.

Carlson, V. J. , Feng, X., & Harwood, R. L. (2004). The "ideal baby": A look at the intersection of temperament and culture. *Zero to Three, 24*(4), 22–28.

Carlson, V. J., & Harwood, R. L. (2000). Understanding and negotiating cultural differences concerning early developmental competence: The six raisin solution. *Zero to Three, 20*(3), 19–23.

Caruso, D. A. (1989). Attachment and exploration in infancy: Research and applied issues. *Early Childhood Research Quarterly, 4*(1), 117–32.

Cassidy, J., & Shaver, P. R. (Eds.). (1999). *Handbook of attachment: Theory, research, and clinical applications* (pp. 713–734). New York: The Guilford Press.

Chang, H. N., Muckelroy, A., & Pulido, D. (1996). *Looking in, looking out: Redefining child care and early education in a diverse society.* San Francisco: California Tomorrow.

Chang, H. N. L., with Pulido, D. (1994). The critical importance of cultural and linguistic continuity for infants and toddlers. *Zero to Three, 15*(2), 13–17.

Chess, S., & Thomas, A. (1987). *Know your child: An authoritative guide for today's parents.* New York: Basic Books.

Cicchetti, D., & Beeghly, M. (1990). *Children with down syndrome.* New York: Cambridge University Press.

Cohen, D., Stern, V., & Balaban, N. (1997). *Observing and recording the behavior of young children* (4th ed.). New York: Teachers College Press.

Corsaro, W. A. (2003). *We're friends, right?: Inside kids' culture.* Washington, DC: Joseph Henry Press.

Corsaro, W. A., & Eder, D. (1990). Children's peer cultures. *Annual Review of Sociology, 16,* 197–220.

Cox, F. M., & Campbell, D. (1968). Young children in a new situation with and without their mothers. *Child Development, 39*(1), 123–32.

Curry, N. E., & Tittnich, E. M. (1972). *Ready or not here we come: The dilemma of school readiness.* (Rev. ed.). Pittsburgh: Pittsburgh University, Arsenal Family and Children's Center. (ERIC Document Reproduction Service No. ED 168 729)

Daley, S. (1982, September 14). Schools open, and 904,000 make the best of it. *New York Times,* p. B3.

Daniel, J. E. (1993). Infants to toddlers: Qualities of effective transitions. *Young Children, 48*(6), 18–21.

Doris, J., McIntyre, A., Kelsey, C., & Lehman, E. (1971). *Separation anxiety and adjustment to nursery school.* Paper presented at the 79th annual meeting of the American Psychological Association, Washington, D.C.

Dozier, M., Albus, K. E., Stovall, K. C., & Bates, B. (2001). Attachment for infants in foster care: The role of caregiver state of mind. *Child Development, 72*(5), 1467–1478.

Dozier, M. E., Dozier, D., & Manni, M. (2002). Attachment and biobehavioral catch-up: The ABC's of helping infants in foster care cope with early adversity. *Zero to Three, 22*(5), 7–13.

Edson, A. (1994). Crossing the great divide: The nursery school child goes to kindergarten. *Young Children, 49*(5), 69–75.

Eheart, B. K., & Zimmerman, C. T. (1998). Hope for the children: Finding discontinuity in foster care. *Zero to Three, 18*(6), 21–26.

Elicker, J., & Fortner-Wood, C. (1995). Adult-child relationships in early childhood programs. *Young Children, 51*(1), 69–78.

Elliot, E. (2003). Challenging our assumptions: Helping a baby to adjust to center care. *Young Children, 58*(4), 22–28.

Erickson, M. F., & Kirz-Riemer, K. (1999). *Infants, toddlers, and families: A framework for support and intervention.* New York: The Guilford Press.

Erikson, E. (1963). *Childhood and society* (Rev. Ed.). New York: W. W. Norton.

Fein, G. G. (1995). Infants in group care: Patterns of despair and detatchment. *Early Childhood Research Quarterly, 10*(3), 261–275.

Foley, G. (1986). Emotional development of children with handicaps. In N. Curry (Ed.)., *The feeling child: Affective development reconsidered* (pp. 57–73). New York: Haworth Press.

Franklin, J. B. (1983, May). Conscious fathering . . . a new look at daddy. *New Frontier, 7,* 10.

Freud, A. (1965). *Normality and pathology in childhood.* New York: International Universities Press.

Furman, E. (1974). *A child's parent dies: Studies in childhood bereavement.* New Haven: Yale University Press.

Furman, R. A. (1972). Experiences in nursery school consultations. In K. Baker (Ed.), *Ideas that work with young children.* Washington, DC: National Association for the Education of Young Children.

Gonzalez-Mena, J. (2005). *Diversity in early care and education: Honoring differences* (4th Ed.). New York: McGraw-Hill.

Greenacre, P. (1957). The childhood of the artist: Libidinal phase development and giftedness. In R. Eissler, A. Freud, H. Hartmann, & E. Kris (Eds.), *The psychoanalytic study of the child* (Vol. 12, pp. 27–72). New York: International Universities Press.

Greenman, J. (1988). *Caring spaces, learning places: Children's environments that work.* Redmond, WA: Exchange Press.

Hains, A. H., Rosenkoetter, S. E., & Fowler, S. A. (1991). Transition planning with families in early intervention programs. *Infants and Young Children, 3*(4), 38–47.

Harwood, R., & Miller, J. G. (1991). Perceptions of attachment behavior: A comparison of Anglo and Puerto Rican mothers. *Merrill-Palmer Quarterly, 37*(4), 583–599.

Hock, E., McKenry, P. C., Hock, M. D., Triolo, S., & Stewart, L. (1980). Child's school entry: A stressful event in the lives of fathers. *Family Relations, 29*(4), 467–72.

Howes, C. (1988). Attachment and child care: Relationships with mother and caregiver. *Early Childhood Research Quarterly, 3*(4), 403–16.

Howes, C. (1988). *Peer interaction of young children.* Monographs of the Society for Research in Child Development, No. 217, *53*(1).

Howes, C. (2000). Social development, family, and attachment relationships of infants and toddlers: Research into practice. In D. Cryer & T. Harms (Eds.), *Infants and toddlers in out-of-home care* (pp. 87–113). Baltimore: Paul H. Brookes.

Jalongo, M. R. (1983). Using crisis-oriented books with young children. *Young Children, 38*(5), 29–35.

Johnston, L., & Mermin, J. (1994). Easing children's entry to school: Home visits help. *Young Children, 49*(5), 62–68.

Kaplan, L. J. (1978). *Oneness and separateness: From infant to individual.* New York: Simon & Schuster.

Karen, R. (1994). *Becoming attached: Unfolding the mystery of the infant-motherbond and its impact on later life*. New York: Warner Books.

Katz, L. (1977). The enabling model in early childhood programs. In L. Katz (Ed.), *Talks with teachers: Reflections on early childhood education* (pp. 49–55). Washington, D.C.: National Association for the Education of Young Children.

Kessler, J. W., Ablon, G., & Smith, E. (1969). Separation reactions in young, mildly retarded children. *Children, 16*(1), 2–7.

Kestenberg-Amigi, J. (2004). Contact and connection: A cross-cultural look at parenting styles in Bali and the United States. *Zero to Three, 24*(5), 32–39.

Klaus, M. H., & Kennell, J. H. (1976). *Maternal infant bonding*. St. Louis: C. V. Mosby Co.

Klaus, M. H., & Kennell, J. H. (1982). *Parent-infant bonding* (2nd ed.). St. Louis: C. V. Mosby Co.

Kleiman, D. (1980, September 9). First school day: A day of doubts and discovery. *New York Times*, p.B1.

Klein, T., Bittel, C., & Molnar, J. (1993). No place to call home: Supporting the needs of homeless children in the early childhood classroom. *Young Children, 48*(6), 22–31.

Ladd, G. W. (1990). Having friends, keeping friends, making friends, and being liked by peers in the classroom: Predictors of children's early school adjustment? *Child Development, 61*(4), 1081–1100.

Lally, J. R. (1995). The impact of child care policies and practices on infant/toddler identity formation. *Young Children, 51*(1), 58–67.

Lamb, M. E. (1981). *Fathers and child development: An integrative overview*. In M. E. Lamb (Ed.), *The role of the father in child development*, (Rev. ed., pp. 1–70). New York: John Wiley.

Lamb, M. E. (1982). Early contact and maternal-infant bonding: One decade later. *Pediatrics, 70*(5), 763–68.

Lamb, M. E. (1997). *The role of the father in child development* (3rd Ed.). New York: John Wiley.

Lamb, M. E., & Hwang, C. P. (1982). Maternal attachment and mother-neonate bonding: A critical review. In M. E. Lamb & A. Brown (Eds.), *Advances in developmental psychology* (Vol. 2, pp. 1–39). Hillsdale, NJ: Erlbaum.

Levine, J., & Pittinsky, T. (1997). *Working fathers: New strategies for balancing work and family*. Reading, MA: Addison-Wesley.

Lieberman, A. F. (1993). *The emotional life of the toddler*. New York: The Free Press.

Lubell, S. (2001, September 2). Overcoming school bus jitters. *New York Times*, p. 4 WE.

Mahler, M. S., Pine, F., & Bergman, A. (1975). *The psychological birth of the human infant: Symbiosis and individuation*. New York: Basic Books.

Maxwell, K. L., & Eller, S. K. (1994). Children's transition to kindergarten. *Young Children, 49*(6), 56–68.

McDonald, L., Kyselka, G. M., & Siebert, P. (1989). Parent perspectives: Transition to preschool. *Teaching Exceptional Children, 22*(1), 4–8.

Meier, D., & Schafran, A. (1999). Strengthening the preschool-to-kindergarten transition: A community collaborates. *Young Children, 54*(3), 40–46.

Paley, V. (2004). *A child's work: The importance of fantasy play.* Chicago: University of Chicago Press.

Parke, R. D., & Amin, A. B. (1999). *Throwaway dads: The myths and barriers that keep men from being the fathers they want to be.* Boston: Houghton Mifflin.

Paul, E. (1975). *A study of the relationship between separation and field dependency in a group of three year old nursery school children.* Unpublished masters thesis, Bank Street College of Education, New York.

Pianta, R. C., & Cox, M. J. (Eds). (1999). *The transition to kindergarten.* Baltimore: Paul Brookes.

Pianta, R. C., & Kraft-Sayre, M. (1999). Parents' observations about their children's transitions to kindergarten. *Young Children, 54*(3), 47–52.

Pianta, R. C., Kraft-Sayre, M., Rimm-Kaufman, S., Gercke, N., & Higgins, T. (2001). Collaboration in building partnerships between families and schools: The National Center for Early Development and Learning in Kindergarten Transition Intervention. *Early Childhood Research Quarterly, 16*(1), 117–132.

Porges, S. W. (2004). Neuroception: A subconscious system for detecting threats and safety. *Zero to Three, 24*(5), 19–24.

Pruett, K. (2000). *Fatherneed: Why father care is as essential as mother care for your child.* New York: Free Press.

Raikes, H. (1996). A secure base for babies: Applying attachment concepts to the infant care setting. *Young Children, 51*(5), 59–67.

Resch, R. C. (1975). *Separation: Natural observations in the first three years of life in an infant day care unit.* Unpublished doctoral dissertation, New York University.

Resch, R. (1977). On separating as a developmental phenomenon: A natural study. *Psychoanalytic Contemporary Science, 5*, 197–269.

Rheingold, H. L., & Eckerman, C. O. (1971). Departures from the mother. In H. R. Schaffer (Ed.), *The origins of human social relations* (pp. 73–82). New York: Academic Press.

Rodriguez, D. T., & Hignett, W. F. (1981). Infant day care: How very young children adapt. *Children Today, 10*(6), 10–12.

Rosenkoetter, S. E., & Rosenkoetter, L. I. (1993, March 28). *Starting school: Perceptions of parents of children with and without disabilities.* Paper presented at Society for Research in Child Development, New Orleans, LA. (ERIC Document Information No. ED356902)

Schaffer, H. R., & Emerson, D. E. (1964). The development of social attachments in infancy. *Monographs of the Society for Research in Child Development, 24*(3, serial no. 94).

Schore, A. (2001). The effects of a secure attachment relationship on right brain development, affect regulation, and infant mental health. *Infant Mental Health Journal, 22*(1–2), 7–66.

Selman, R. L., & Selman, A. P. (1979, October). Children's ideas about friendship: A new theory. *Psychology Today,* 71–80, 114.

Singer, L. M., Brodzinsky, D. M., Ramsay, D., Steir, M., & Waters, E. (1985). Mother-infant attachment in adoptive families. *Child Development, 56*(6), 1543–1551.

Small, F. (1983). "Give me to warble spontaneous songs . . .": Using spontaneity to develop a therapeutic music program. Unpublished masters thesis, Bank Street College of Education, New York.

Small, M. (1998). *Our babies ourselves: How biology and culture shape the way we parent*. New York: Anchor Books.

Smolkin, L. B. (1999). The practice of effective transitions: Players who make a winning team. In Pianta, R. C., & Cox, M. J. (Eds.). (1999). *The transition to kindergarten* (pp. 325–350). Baltimore: Paul Brookes.

Speers, R. N., McFarland, M. B., Arnaud, S., & Curry, N. E. (1971). Recapitulation of separation-individuation processes when the normal three-year-old enters nursery school. In J. B. McDevitt & C. F. Settlage (Eds.), *Separation-individuation: Essays in honor of Margaret S. Mahler*. New York: International Universities Press.

Steig, W. (1971). *Amos and Boris*. New York: Farrar, Straus & Giroux.

Stern, D. (1985). *The interpersonal world of the infant: A view from psychoanalysis and development psychology*. New York: Basic Books.

Szamreta, J. M. (2003). Peekaboo power to ease separation and build secure relationships. *Young Children, 58*(1), 88–94.

Wachs, T. D. (2004). Temperament and development: The role of context in biologically based system. *Zero to Three, 24*(4), 12–21.

Wehmiller, P. L. (2002). *A gathering of gifts*. New York: Church Publishing.

White, R. W. (1968). Motivation reconsidered: The concept of competence. In M. Almy (Ed.), *Early childhood play: Selected academic readings* (pp. WITE 1A–37A). New York: Associated Educational Services Corp.

Winnicott, D. W. (1957). *Mother and child: A primer of first relationships*. New York: Basic Books.

Wong-Fillmore, L. (1991). When learning a second language means losing the first. *Early Childhood Research Quarterly, 6*(3), 323–346.

Young-Bruehl, E., & Bethelard, F. (2000). *Cherishment: A psychology of the heart*. New York: Free Press.

Zelle, R. S., & Coyner, A. B. (1983). *Developmentally disabled infants and toddlers: Assessment and intervention*. Philadephia: F. A. Davie Co.

Zill, N. (1999). Promoting educational equity and excellence in kindergarten. In R. C. Pianta & M. J. Cox (Eds.), *The transition to kindergarten* (pp. 67–105). Baltimore: Paul Brookes.

Index

Abandonment, feelings of, 65
Ablon, G., 66
Acting out, 26
Adams, S. A., 26
Adoptive parents, 17
Ainsworth, M.D.S., 18, 53
Albus, K. E., 17, 26
Amae, 18
Amin, A. B., 101
Appearance-disappearance theme, 50.
    See also Hide-and-seek; Peek-a-
    boo
"Approach-avoidance" games, 81
Arnaud, S., 33
Arsenian, J. M., 93
Attachment
    as basic necessity for development,
        112
    and brain, 22
    definition of, 17
    development of, 20–24
    between fathers and children, 100
    and feelings about starting early
        care and education, 6
    and meanings of separation, 25, 26
    to peers, 80
    and policies for entry and
        separation, 112–22
    and preparation for entering
        program, 86
    quality of, 20–21
    as at roots of separation feelings,
        17–20
    and social life of classrooms, 80

and special needs children, 66
and using curriculum to cope with
    separation, 66, 80
Authority, challenging of, 81, 93
Avoidance, of parents, 52, 53

Badness, 49
Balaban, N., 56
Ball play, 73
Barclay, C., 93
Bates, B., 17, 64–65
Beeghly, M., 66
Behavior
    adult behaviors that help children
        cope with separation, 68–69
    and coping through play, 46–52
    and feelings about starting early
        care and education, 3–4, 11
    and how observations can help, 55–
        57
    and increased dependence, 41
    learning from children's, 29–57
    and relationships with other
        children, 45–46
    and reunions with parents, 52–53
    and using curriculum to cope with
        separation, 64–65
    See also specific behavior
Bell, S. M., 5, 18
Belligerence, 45, 46
Berger, E. H., 96
Bergman, A., 7–8, 21–23, 24
Bernhardt, J. L., 7
Bethelard, F., 18

143

About the Author

NANCY BALABAN has been on the faculty of Bank Street College Graduate School of Education for many years, involved in educating graduate students in both early childhood education and infant and parent development and early intervention. She received her doctorate from New York University, her master's from Bank Street College, and an undergraduate degree from Wellesley College. She has an extensive background as an early childhood teacher. A speaker and writer of many articles and book chapters, she is coauthor of *Observing Recording the Behavior of Young Children* with Dorothy Cohen and Virginia Stern.